# The Great Oil Price Fixes

## and how to trade them

Simon Watkins

 BOOKS

*This book is dedicated to my son, James Harper-Watkins*

# CONTENTS

# Key Players And Fixes
# In The Great Oil Game

Over the past few years, there have been a slew of accusations from media, regulators and participants of varying degrees of manipulation of markets, especially those relating to equities and FX. For the good trader, though, none of these supposed practices should have affected their ability either to maximise profits or minimise losses to any meaningful degree whatsoever, given that they should have been using intelligent risk management parameters (see *Risk Management And Hedging* section), dynamic cross-asset class investment techniques (see *Trading Oil And Gas Market Correlations* section), and the optimal mix of technical analysis (see *Technical Analysis* section) and macro-economic factors (see later) that have been vital to success for as long as markets have existed.

However, **the oil market** – a term used here as a synonym for the petroleum market (which covers both naturally occurring unprocessed crude oil and petroleum products that are constituted from refined crude oil) – **is different from all the rest, even other commodities markets. This is because it has been manipulated to an extremely high degree for decades, both overtly and covertly, and will likely continue to be so, given oil's enduring geopolitical importance to the world's supplier and consumer states alike.** It is, in short, simply too important to be left to chance in any significant way.

So, **if a trader knows the essential dynamics that drive the global oil market, it offers unparalleled opportunities to make returns over and above those of other markets, often in a virtually unidirectional manner over time. Understanding the global oil market is also an essential part of being able to trade**

**FX, equities, bonds and other commodities, to their optimal profitability.**

This book is not a history book, but a bit of history is a necessary platform for establishing the broad architecture in which readers can trade this market, together with a solid knowledge of the market-specific trading nuances required in this particular field and the essential elements of the general trading methodology, strategies and tactics that underpin top professional traders.

# The 'Seven Sisters'

**Prior to the formation of OPEC (see below), the global oil market from the early 1940s had been dominated by a Western-centric group of seven major international oil companies (IOCs), known colloquially as the 'Seven Sisters':**

- The Anglo-Persian Oil Company (now BP)
- Gulf Oil
- Standard Oil of California (SoCal)
- Texaco (now Chevron)
- Royal Dutch Shell
- Standard Oil of New Jersey (now Esso)
- Standard Oil Company of New York (Socony, and now ExxonMobil).

**Until the onset of the 1973 Oil Crisis (see below) these firms controlled together around 85% of the world's petroleum reserves,** having often paid the host countries a minimal percentage of the resulting sales profits in return, and sometimes – as in the case of the world's top oil producer, Saudi Arabia – having procured initial exploration rights for virtually nothing (the US's Standard Oil paid the Saudis just USD275,000 in April 1933 for the rights to drill across the entire country).

**The Great Seven Sisters Fixes**

**The Seven Sisters' fixes were – unlike OPEC's have proven – often unilateral and designed to increase one company's market share at the expense of another's.** Although in 1959, for example, the IOCs reduced the posted price for Venezuelan crude by USD0.05 per barrel (pb) and then by USD0.25 pb, and that for Middle Eastern crude by USD0.18 pb (without consulting the host countries), in August 1960 Standard Oil (again with no warning to its suppliers) announced a cut of up to 7% of the posted prices of Middle Eastern crude oils (see more on this fix in later chapters).

# OPEC

In 1960, OPEC (the Organization of the Petroleum Exporting Countries) was **specifically founded to 'co-ordinate and unify the petroleum policies' of all of its member states; i.e. to align them and, consequently, to fix the oil price.** Membership of this cartel comprises virtually all of the world's major oil and gas suppliers – in alphabetical order, not that of global oil significance: Algeria, Angola, Ecuador, Iran, Iraq, Kuwait, Libya, Nigeria, Qatar, Saudi Arabia, the United Arab Emirates (UAE) and Venezuela – with the most notable exception, perhaps, being Russia.

**World's Largest Proved Reserve Holders Of Crude Oil, Current (billion barrels)**

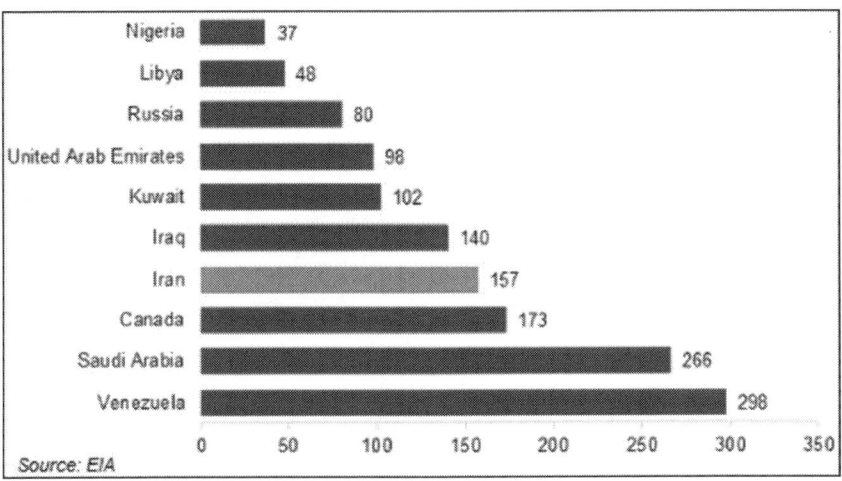

Source: EIA

Although there are members that flout OPEC guidance, **this club sets the oil production targets of its members. With a collective 40% or so of the world's crude oil output produced by these countries and around 60% of the total petroleum traded internationally coming from their oil exports, what OPEC says and does plays a huge part in determining the global price not just of oil but of natural gas and related oil and gas products.** Obviously, in the most basic terms, if OPEC cuts oil production – all other factors remaining equal – then the price of oil and related products will rise, and if it increases output then the price will fall, according to the usual laws of supply and demand.

## The First Great OPEC (Saudi) Fix

Until 1973, the basis of the historical relationship between the US and OPEC (entirely driven at that point by Saudi Arabia) had been demarcated at a meeting on 14 February 1945 between then American President Franklin D Roosevelt and the Saudi King at the time, Abdulaziz. The first face-to-face contact between the two, it was held on board the US Navy cruiser Quincy in the Great Bitter Lake segment of the Suez Canal. The deal to which they agreed, which persisted unchallenged until 1973, was this: **the US would get all of the oil and gas supplies it needed for as long as Saudi had hydrocarbons reserves, in return for which the US would guarantee the security both of the country and of the ruling House of Saud.**

Having said all of this, **the key moment that would define the global oil market as it still stands today was the 1973 Oil Crisis.** This began in October of that year when OPEC members plus Egypt, Syria and Tunisia began an embargo on oil exports to the US, the UK, Japan, Canada and the Netherlands in response to the US's supplying of arms to Israel in the Yom Kippur War. By the end of the embargo in March 1974, the price of oil had risen from USD3 pb to nearly USD12 pb. As the Saudi Minister of Oil and Mineral Reserves at the time, Sheikh Ahmed Zaki Yamani unequivocally highlighted at that point, the extremely negative effects on the global economy marked a fundamental shift in the world balance of power between the developing nations that produced oil and the developed industrial nations that consumed it (see more on this fix in later chapters).

# Saudi Arabia

Ten years ago Saudi Arabia was the undisputed king of the global energy complex – the world's 'swing' producer – sitting atop OPEC, propped up by its own massive high quality oil reserves (see chart below) and able to extend its petro-powered influence into all areas of the world's economy; from the trajectory of the US dollar, through the price of gold, to the performance of the leading equities indices. **From 2004 to now (2015), the oil price has to varying degrees been the product of the tune played from the pied pipes of Saudi:** rising from around USD50 pb of West Texas Intermediate

(WTI) at the end of 2004, through the USD147 pb level in 2008 and back down again in 2014/15 to around the USD50 pb.

However, **underlying the simple price movements, the global energy market has undergone fundamental complex changes (see below) that have cast doubts over Saudi's stature in the oil markets in the years to come, not just from the US-driven threat from shale oil and gas nor from the increased geopolitical tensions in the Middle East as a whole but also from questions about precisely how much oil Saudi actually has** and consequently its ability to act effectively as a swing energy producer by manipulating its spare capacity.

**Global Crude Oil Quality, By Types**

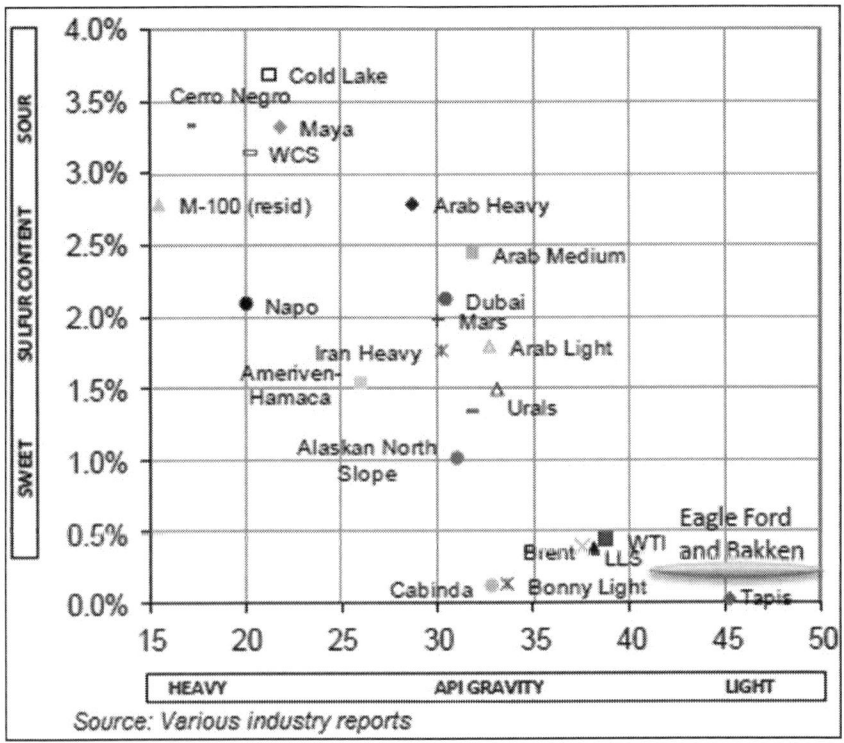

*Source: Various industry reports*

*[Chart Key:*

*The petroleum industry classifies crude oil by three general parameters:*

*1. Its API (American Petroleum Institute) gravity (a measure of density) = horizontal axis label. Light crude has over 31.1 degrees API, medium has 22.3-31.1 degrees API, heavy has below 22.3 degrees API and extra heavy has under 10 degrees API, although definitions do vary slightly depending on the organisation involved. Light trades at a premium to the others as it produces a higher yield of petrol and is less difficult and costly to refine*

*2. Its sulphur content = vertical axis label. Sweet crude oil has less than 0.5% sulphur content and sour more than 0.5%. Sweet trades at a premium to sour, as it requires less refining to meet international sulphur emissions standards*

*3. Its broad geographic location = points plotted within the body of the chart. There are basically three global benchmarks for oil pricing, all of which are light and sweet: West Texas Intermediate (WTI), Brent and the average of the Dubai and Oman crudes]*

According to the US's Energy Information Administration (EIA), Saudi Arabia had approximately 266 billion barrels (bbbl) of proved oil reserves, in addition to half of the 2.5 bbbl estimated in the Saudi-Kuwaiti shared Partitioned Neutral Zone as of 1 January 2015, over half of which is held in eight longstanding fields; 16% of total proved world oil reserves. However, **oil and gas (hydrocarbons) reserves figures are often nowadays a matter more of political expediency than of cold reality, with doubt over the veracity of any figures produced anywhere having grown in recent years, but especially perhaps in the Middle East.** For example, Abu Dhabi claimed reserves of 92.3 bbbl from 1988 to 2004 but, over that period, approximately 14 bbbl were extracted. Similarly, back in 1989, Saudi Arabia claimed to be sitting on a total of 170 bbbl of oil but, only a year later and without the discovery of any major new oil fields, the official reserve estimate somehow grew by 51.2% to 257 bbbl.

## Saudi Arabia's Major Oil And Gas Infrastructure

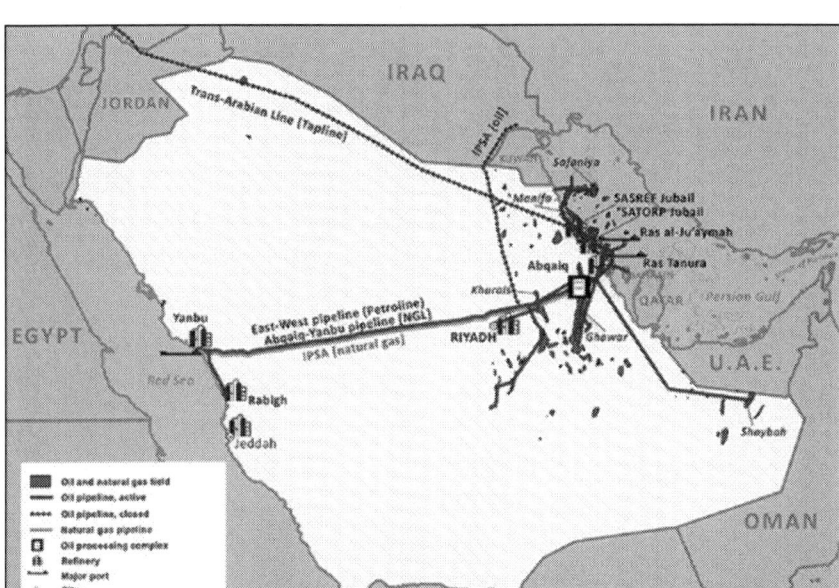

Source: EIA

The country has often stated that it has a spare capacity of between 2-2.5 million barrels per day (mbpd), with the capability to ramp up its production to about 12.5 mbpd in the event of unexpected disruptions elsewhere. However, it is very unlikely that it could pump at these levels for a sustained period of time, and this idea has been supported by comments from Gulf officials at OPEC, which stated in the midst of Iraqi supply fears that Saudi Arabia could ramp-up output by another 1-1.3 mbpd in a best case scenario. Officials also mentioned that production of 11.5 mbpd is untested and could only be maintained for a very short period and that, in any event, higher production would be very difficult and would require producing heavy crudes. In addition, it has been noted that the country's rising domestic consumption, notably to power its growing electricity generation networks and transport sector, has been eating into its crude export potential. Despite Saudi Arabia's heavy focus on developing its gas resources to support its crude export growth, it is expected that the slow development will be insufficient to offset rampant growth in demand for electricity leaving a heavy reliance on oil.

Combined with growing electricity demand, Saudi Aramco's aggressive expansion of its downstream sector (relating to the refining of crude oil and the processing and purifying of natural gas and the resulting products, including gasoline) will put further pressure on domestic consumption in the coming years. Indeed, there is likely to be average oil consumption growth of 7% per year across the next 10 years, which compares to average oil production growth of just 1% (albeit from a higher base) over the same period. This has already reduced the country's spare oil production capacity and will continue to do so progressively, so reducing its ability to manipulate the global oil price and, as a corollary of this, its geopolitical power.

## The Second (Current) Great OPEC (Saudi) Fix

'Power is in the production' is an old adage in the trading markets, meaning dealers making the most money have the most say in how things are run, and in the oil industry it appears no less potent. **It is little surprise, then, to see that the Saudis' voice in OPEC has become increasingly less compelling for other cartel members over the past 10 years, given questions over its reserves numbers (see above).** From the Saudi side as well, as long ago as 2008 there were signs that perhaps the Kingdom was less interested in holding onto its dominant power in OPEC. In September of that year it publically announced that it would not honour the cartel's guidance on production, even walking out of OPEC meetings, effectively saying that it would deal with changes in market demand as and when they arose.

**In October 2014 during private meetings in New York between Saudi officials and other senior figures in the global oil industry, the Saudis appeared to reveal that the Kingdom – far from looking to keep prices high (as had been the normal**

inclination of OPEC for many years, as mentioned above, in order to boost the prosperity of OPEC member states) – was willing to tolerate Brent prices between USD80-USD90/bbl for a period of 1-2 years (through increasing production) in order to achieve two aims:

1. To destroy or at least slow progress in the developing shale energy industry (especially that of the fast-moving US).
2. To pressure other OPEC members to contribute to supply discipline.

This marked a significant divergence from the acceptable range of prices previously stated by Saudi Oil Minister Ali al-Naimi as being 'USD100, USD110, USD95,' and comments later that year that Saudi was not at all concerned even if oil prices fell to USD20/bbl (see more on this fix in later chapters).

In respect of the latter objective, there will always be those members who for various country-specific reasons will continue to breach OPEC production guidance. In terms of the latter, meanwhile, some indicators have emerged showing that a degree of slowdown in the development of the shale energy industry may be taking place. For example, the US oil rig count in January/February 2015 saw its biggest period-on-period fall since 1991, and the gas rig count has fallen substantially as well.

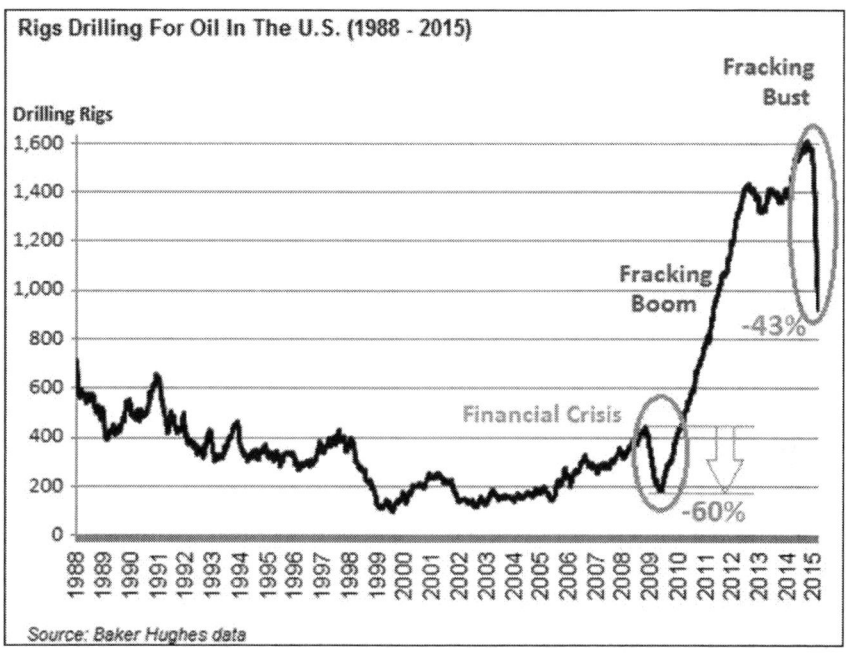

Rigs Drilling For Oil In The U.S. (1988 - 2015)

Source: Baker Hughes data

According to industry figures **as at the end of the first quarter of 2015, around one third of the 800 oil and gas projects (worth USD500 billion and totalling nearly 60 billion barrels of oil equivalent) scheduled for final investment decisions (FID) this year are 'unconventional', meaning that around USD150 billion of shale projects could be cancelled or postponed.** Already, notable retrenchments include French energy giant, Total, recently deciding to postpone the FID on the Joslyn project in Alberta, Canada (estimated cost USD11 billion). Additionally, Royal Dutch Shell's (RDS) liquefied natural gas (LNG) project in British Columbia requires oil at USD80/bbl to break even and RDS' Chief Financial Officer, Henry Simon, indicated in October 2014 that it was "less likely" to go ahead with unconventional projects in West Canada if oil fell below USD80/bbl. Even in the US-centric Gulf of Mexico, one of the most attractive oil production areas in the world, projects are facing challenges. BP last year put on hold a decision on its 'Mad Dog Phase 2' deep water project in the Gulf after its development costs ballooned to USD20 billion and further delays on the field's development are expected by analysts.

In sum, **any offshore project with a development cost above USD30pb would most likely be put on hold at current oil prices.** Similarly, many Australian LNG firms require spot oil prices between the USD75-90/bbl level in order to generate a 10% rate of return, so some of these projects could – at the very least – be substantially delayed. In this context, Woodside Petroleum's chief executive officer Peter Coleman said in a speech in November 2014 that a prolonged oil price slump will hurt returns at existing LNG projects and threaten future developments, presumably placing at risk its target of approving the USD35 billion Browse LNG project in the second half of 2015.

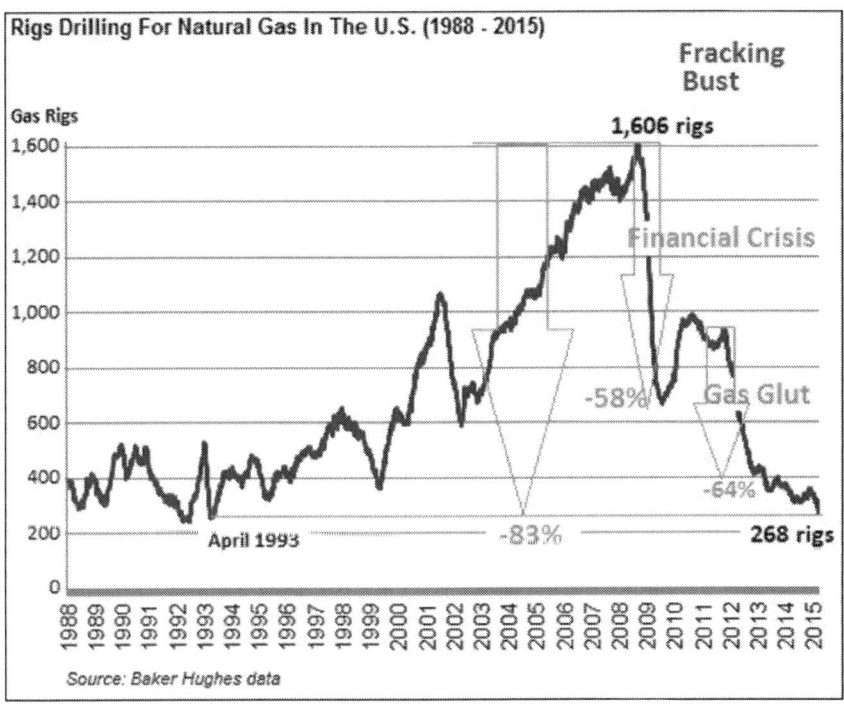

# The US

Given the huge economic and reputational damage done to the US as a result of the quadrupling of oil prices due to the Saudis' 1973 oil embargo, **the US Congress banned exports of oil to destinations outside the Americas from the country, despite its producing many millions of barrels of oil per day at that time, in order to make it more energy self-sufficient (or at least, not so dependent on the Saudis for energy).** Indeed, the US has been a major petroleum product supplier to the Americas for the past decade: in 2003, it exported 0.6 mbpd of petroleum products to other countries in the Americas, primarily Mexico and Canada; and, just 10 years later, US exports to the region totalled 2.0 mbpd, still primarily to Mexico and Canada but increasingly to other countries, most notably Brazil and Chile.

Companies were allowed to export refined fuel to other regions, such as gasoline and diesel, but not oil itself until last year when the US Commerce Department, which oversees the Bureau of Industry and Security, is believed to have changed the definition of some ultra-light oil, clearing the way for two companies (Pioneer Natural Resources of Irving, Texas and Enterprise Products Partners of Houston, Texas) to sell abroad, although the ban on straight US crude remains in place.

Overall, the US has become an oil producer on the same scale as Saudi Arabia, with EIA data showing that combined production of crude oil and lease condensate rose from 5.7 mbpd in 2011 to 7.4 mbpd in 2013 and the agency's 'Short-Term Energy Outlook' projecting production in 2015 reaching 9.2 mbpd, around 9.6 mbpd between 2017 and 2020 (close to its historical high of 9.6 mbpd in 1970) and growth perhaps continuing through the 2020s and into the 2030s, with production reaching 13.3 mbpd in 2036.

## US Crude Oil Production, By Crude Type (million barrels per day)

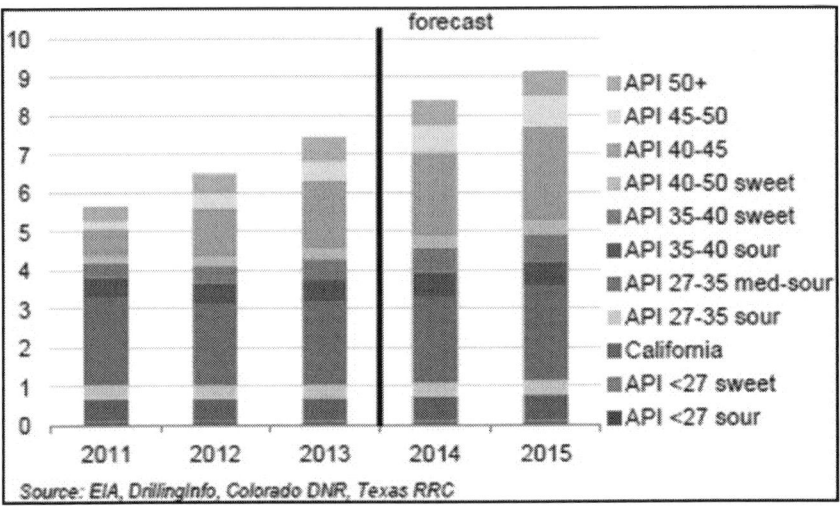

*[Chart Key: See above for API and Sweet and Sour definitions]*

More recently, though, **the US has looked again at further reducing both its energy and economic dependence on oil and gas producers in the Middle East by developing its huge shale oil (also referred to as 'tight' or 'light tight' oil) resources (and its gas resources),** which consist of light crude oil contained in petroleum-bearing formations of low permeability that are extracted via hydraulic fracturing and horizontal well drilling.

**Technically Recoverable Shale Oil And Gas Resources Against Total World Resources**

| | Crude oil (billion barrels) | Wet natural gas (trillion cubic feet) |
|---|---|---|
| **Outside the United States** | | |
| Shale oil and shale gas | 287 | 6,634 |
| Non-shale | 2,847 | 13,817 |
| Total | 3,134 | 20,451 |
| Increase in total resources due to inclusion of shale oil and shale gas | 10% | 48% |
| Shale as a percent of total | 9% | 32% |
| **United States** | | |
| Shale / tight oil and shale gas | 58 | 665 |
| Non-shale | 164 | 1,766 |
| Total | 223 | 2,431 |
| Increase in total resources due to inclusion of shale oil and shale gas | 35% | 38% |
| Shale as a percent of total | 26% | 27% |
| **Total World** | | |
| Shale / tight oil and shale gas | 345 | 7,299 |
| Non-shale | 3,012 | 15,583 |
| Total | 3,357 | 22,882 |
| Increase in total resources due to inclusion of shale oil and shale gas | 11% | 47% |
| Shale as a percent of total | 10% | 32% |
| *Source: EIA* | | |

**With the vast shale oil and gas reserves held by the US and other non-Middle East (and non-OPEC) countries, this energy resource had been widely tipped as being a stunning game-changer for the global energy market, with a corollary shift in geopolitical power that this implies.** This remains the case, albeit with two important caveats: there are wide discrepancies of shale oil resources recoverable both from different deposits and even within a single deposit itself, and the 'unconventional' extraction costs for shale oil are much higher than for oil retrieved by 'conventional methods'.

This means that **the lower the oil price, the less point there is for IOCs to try to exploit such shale oil deposits and the more the world economy will continue to depend on traditional sources of oil; that is, OPEC producers in general and producers from the Middle East in particular.**

This is the basis of the current oil price fix being waged by **OPEC members, under the lead of Saudi Arabia (see above).**

| Top 10 Countries For Technically Recoverable Shale Oil Resources | | | Top 10 Countries For Technically Recoverable Shale Gas Resources | | |
|---|---|---|---|---|---|
| Rank | Country | Shale oil (billion barrels) | Rank | Country | Shale gas (trillion cubic feet) |
| 1 | Russia | 75 | 1 | China | 1,115 |
| 2 | U.S. | 58 | 2 | Argentina | 802 |
| 3 | China | 32 | 3 | Algeria | 707 |
| 4 | Argentina | 27 | 4 | U.S. | 665 |
| 5 | Libya | 26 | 5 | Canada | 573 |
| 6 | Australia | 18 | 6 | Mexico | 545 |
| 7 | Venezuela | 13 | 7 | Australia | 437 |
| 8 | Mexico | 13 | 8 | South Africa | 390 |
| 9 | Pakistan | 9 | 9 | Russia | 285 |
| 10 | Canada | 9 | 10 | Brazil | 245 |
| | World Total | 345 | | World Total | 7,299 |

Source: EIA

# Russia

As can be seen from many of the charts above, **Russia – in the simple terms of oil and gas reserves (both conventional and non-conventional on site) – is a global energy powerhouse,** albeit one that is currently constrained from realising its full potential due to political and economic sanctions related to its activities in Ukraine, but these constraints will not last forever. From a purely strategic standpoint, Ukraine is Russia's soft underbelly as, dominated by Russia, it anchors Russian power across the Carpathian mountains. If Ukraine came under the influence or control of a Western power, Russia's – and Belarus's – southern flank would be wide open along an arc running from the Polish border east almost to Volgograd and then south to the Sea of Azov, a distance of more than 1,000 miles, more than 700 of which lie along Russia proper, with few natural barriers to hinder military advances.

## CEE And FSU Gas Supply Routes

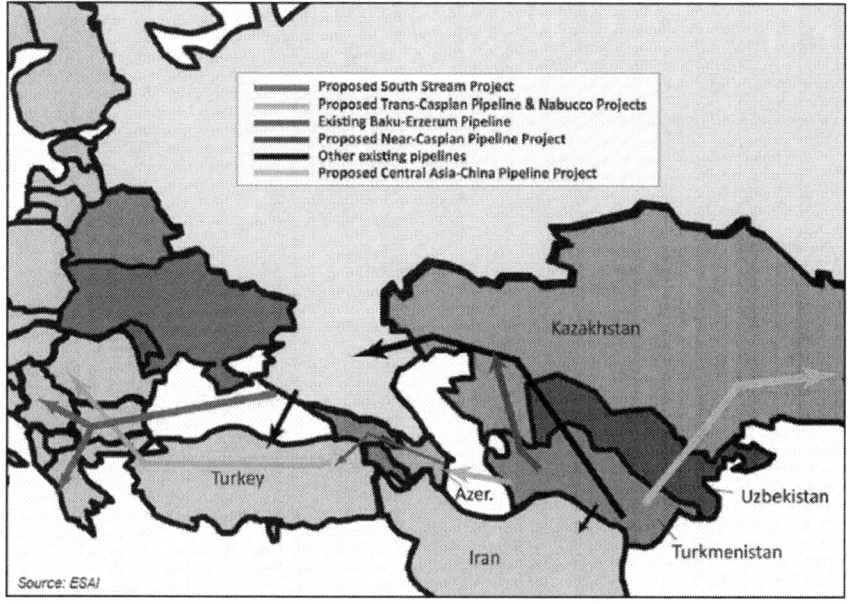

Consequently, short of direct military action against Russia by the West in Ukraine, even with expanded sanctions, Russia is unlikely to alter its rebel-backed occupancy of the strategically-vital eastern Ukraine in 2015. Its intransigence in this respect was underlined very recently in its willingness to play the sanctions game back at the West with its cancellation of the South Stream pipeline project that would have supplied gas directly to Western countries. Instead, by concentrating all such supplies through Ukraine, Russia has underlined the importance of maintaining its foothold in the country in the form of the – massive, but discretionary – tariffs that it charges Ukraine's Naftogaz.

For the area of the world that has for some time been most dependent on imports of Russian energy – the EU – it is interesting to hear senior Russian sources maintain the view that the EU needs Russia at least as much as Russia needs the increasingly fiscally troubled collection of states. For a start, with the EU recording month upon month of zero or near-zero economic growth and energy costs constituting a major chunk of export goods' prices, losing gas supplies from Russia would expose the trade area to having to plug the gaps at emerging energy pricing tariffs, with corollary negative effects on the competitiveness of its exports.

## CEE And FSU Oil Supply Routes

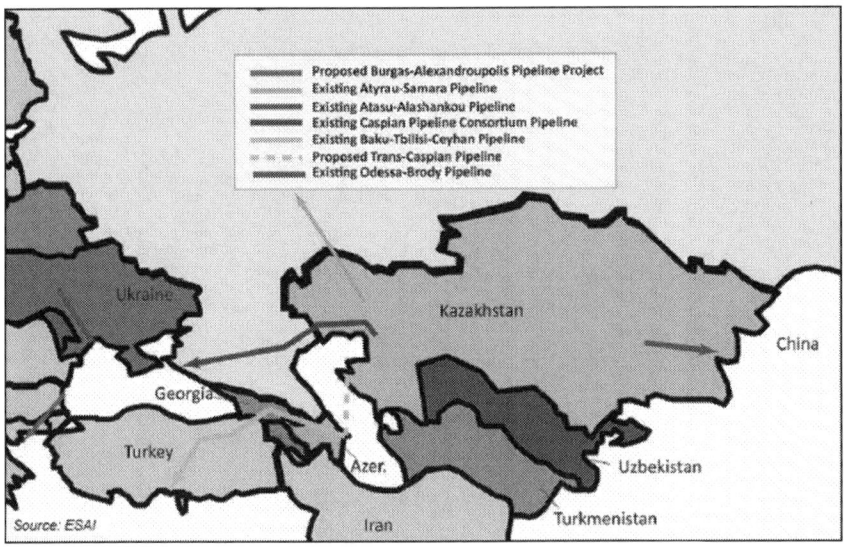

Aside from this, of course, the *de facto* leader of the EU – Germany – is extremely unlikely to back any dramatic increase in sanctions against Russia from the EU, given that Germany sold about EUR36 billion (USD48 billion) of goods to Russia in 2014 and some 6,200 German firms are active there, with around EUR20 billion of investment. Moreover, Germany imports around 35% of its gas from Russia.

On the downside of the outlook, it is true that most of its oil production continues to originate from just one region – West Siberia (particularly from the Priobskoye and Samotlor fields) – and although new projects in the area are under development they may only serve in the long term to offset declining output from some of the region's fields as they age and not in genuinely increased output. On the upside, though, whilst the Sakhalin group of fields in the Far East currently only contributes about 3% of Russia's total production, this area – along with untapped oil reserves in Eastern Siberia and the Russian Arctic – may yield further massive finds of new oil (and gas) reserves, and **there is little doubt – all other factors remaining equal – that Russia will re-emerge, after the current Ukraine-related crisis and sanctions have worked themselves through, as an even greater powerhouse in the global hydrocarbons industry than before.**

# Iran

Iran has until very recently (14 July to be exact) stood in the global hydrocarbons complex in a theoretical position somewhat akin to that of Russia, in that **it has enormous natural resources wealth – perhaps more so ultimately than Moscow – but had been subject to more stringent sanctions for longer (since 1979 in one form or another) than its near neighbour.** The middle of July, though, saw perhaps the most momentous event in the global oil and gas industry in a generation, with the P5+1 group of nations (the US, Russia, China, France, the UK plus Germany) supporting in principle the lifting of sanctions on Iran. This landmark agreement brings back into the global markets one of the richest oil and gas plays in the world, one which offers international oil companies (IOCs) a vast and largely untapped opportunity to get in on the ground floor of exploration, development, and expansion.

**Monthly Iranian Exports Of Crude Oil And Condensate (million barrels per day)**

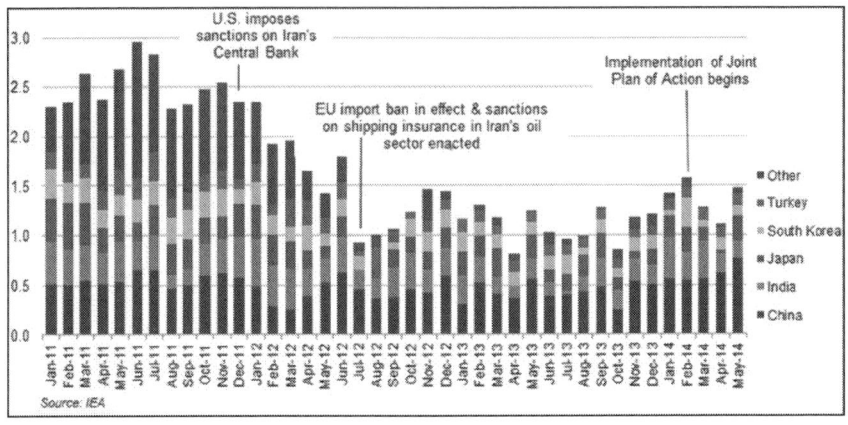

Iran has an estimated 157 billion barrels of proved crude oil reserves, representing nearly 10% of the world's crude oil reserves, 13% of reserves held by OPEC. It ranks as the world's fourth-largest reserve holder of oil and one of its top 10 oil producers. Its oil sector, though, has remained most affected by ongoing sanctions; only a year after the US and the European Union (EU) enacted sanctions measures at the end of 2011 and during the summer of 2012, Iran's net oil and natural gas export revenue dropped by 47% to USD63 billion, and the year after they fell another 11% to USD56 billion, despite gas exports numbers holding steady over the period. However, significant results may be expected this year, as is evidenced, for example, in its development plans for the 900 square kilometre Azadegan oil field, which is split into two sites – North and South. This remains Iran's biggest oil find since the late 1960s, with total estimated reserves of about 42 bbbl, of which around 7 bbbl are deemed recoverable from Iran's side.

Great as its oil reserves are, its gas reserves are even greater, with **Iran having estimated proved natural gas reserves of 1,193 trillion cubic feet (Tcf), second only to Russia, 17% of the world's total proved natural gas reserves and more than one-third of OPEC's reserves.** Additionally, Iran has a high success rate of natural gas exploration, in terms of wildcat drilling, which is estimated at around 80%, compared to the world average success rate of 30-35%. The country also holds a further estimated 2 Tcf of proved and probable natural gas reserves onshore and offshore in the Caspian basin. Its biggest field is its giant South Pars non-associated gas field – a 3,700 sqkm sector of the 9,700 sqkm basin shared with Qatar (in the form of the 6,000 sqkm North Field) – which accounts for around 40% of the country's natural gas reserves (mostly in the southern region in the Gulf) and around 60% of its gas production.

Despite ongoing international sanctions that impact Iran's hydrocarbons exports, a sea-change appears to be afoot in the country's strategy to manage the likely increases in South Pars gas production, with a greater emphasis being laid on plans to direct additional supplies to the international markets rather than the domestic ones, especially in power generation or for oil field reinjection purposes. In this respect, Iran is the world's third largest producer of natural gas – around 170 bcm in 2014, according to Tehran figures – historically behind the US and Russia but ahead of Qatar and Canada; from 2000 to 2010 its output increased at an average annual growth rate of just over 8% (although the past four years has seen this annual growth rate drop to around 5%).

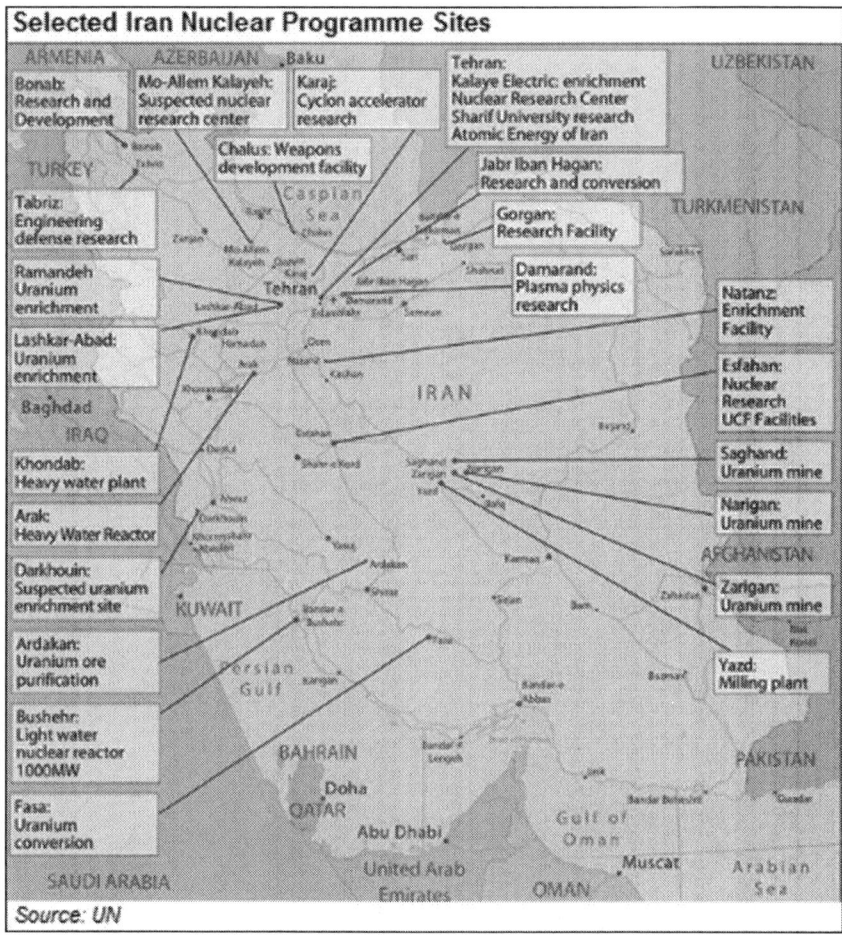

**Selected Iran Nuclear Programme Sites**

Bonab: Research and Development

Mo-Allem Kalayeh: Suspected nuclear research center

Karaj: Cyclon accelerator research

Tehran: Kalaye Electric enrichment Nuclear Research Center Sharif University research Atomic Energy of Iran

Chalus: Weapons development facility

Jabr Iban Hagan: Research and conversion

Tabriz: Engineering defense research

Gorgan: Research Facility

Ramandeh: Uranium enrichment

Damarand: Plasma physics research

Lashkar-Abad: Uranium enrichment

Natanz: Enrichment Facility

Esfahan: Nuclear Research UCF Facilities

Khondab: Heavy water plant

Saghand: Uranium mine

Arak: Heavy Water Reactor

Narigan: Uranium mine

Darkhouin: Suspected uranium enrichment site

Zarigan: Uranium mine

Ardakan: Uranium ore purification

Yazd: Milling plant

Bushehr: Light water nuclear reactor 1000MW

Fasa: Uranium conversion

*Source: UN*

In the context of sanctions, much of Asia (especially China and India and to a lesser degree South Korea and Japan) long ignored them, and there had been increasing signs that the EU was keen to abandon them as well. **The key turning point in this respect came with the revelations by Edward Snowden that Germany was extensively spied on by US intelligence agencies (as were all other major EU states), which led to a breakdown of trust on the German side and an increasing unwillingness to simply toe the US line on all major geopolitical decisions.** A prime example of this newfound German independence from US global policies was seen in the widely-reported deal struck personally between German Chancellor Angela Merkel and Russian President Vladimir Putin. This would have seen Moscow's annexation of Crimea officially recognised in exchange for a USD1 billion compensation package for the Ukraine government (for rent it used to pay for basing its navy at the port of Sevastopol), plus an agreement from Putin not to interfere with Ukraine's new trade relations with the EU, to offer Kiev a long-term contract for future gas supplies with Russian hydrocarbons behemoth Gazprom and to withdraw its support for rebels fighting in eastern Ukraine. Interestingly as an adjunct to this, in September 2014, a senior figure involved in developing EU energy strategy said: "Iran is far towards the top of our priorities for mid-term measures that will help reduce our reliance on Russian gas supplies."

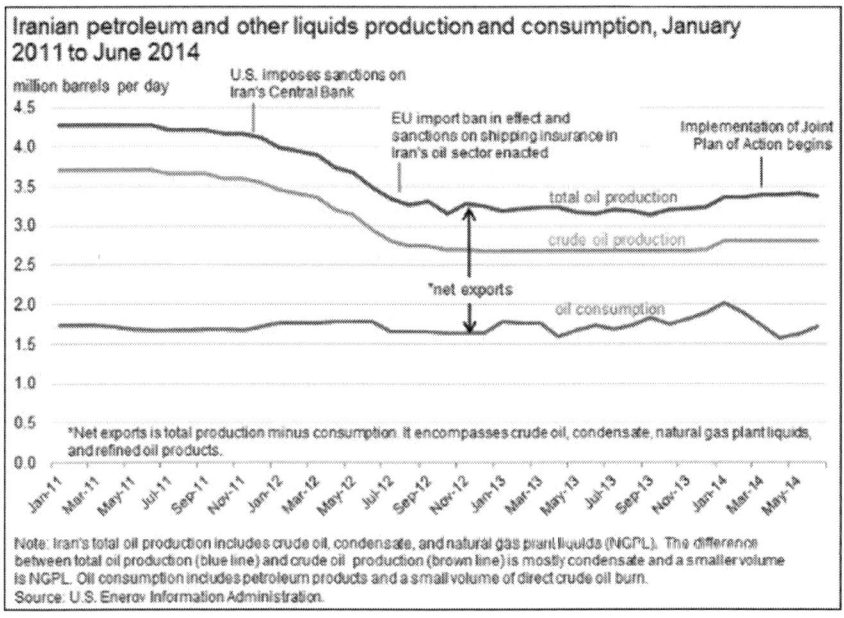

In terms of pure economic opportunity cost as well, **Germany did not want to end up with the leftovers from the freeing up of Iran's vast hydrocarbon resources, after the US itself lifted sanctions at some point in the future, as it did with the Iraqi oil**

**and gas industry.** In this context, the US's *modus operandi* was always the same in these situations; which is positioning its companies and advisers within the integrated architecture of a country's oil and gas industry before it frees the industry up, then taking the lion's share of all of the assets. **In the case of Iran, the US would be looking to secure around USD150 billion of revenue within just the first few years, and Germany – and the EU – was never likely to allow that to happen again.**

This said, **despite Iran's massive hydrocarbons wealth, the negative price effect on the already depressed oil market is likely to be limited for some considerable period after the deal was signed.** In general terms, although the Iranians have said that they can increase production by 1 million barrels per day immediately, there have been very little modern investments and upgrades to the Iranian oil fields since 1979, and any oilman will attest to the fact that a producer cannot shut a well for years and years then simply turn a wrench and have oil flows aplenty as though no break in output has occurred. More specifically, trader talk of the impact of the amount of Iranian oil in storage as of end-June 2015 – the 50 million or so barrels of crude and condensates (including around 40 million barrels of crude oil, according to maritime data and analytics company Windward) aboard tankers in the Persian Gulf – suddenly being released onto the international oil markets appears significantly overplayed. **Now that the deal has been struck, these barrels are likely to come onto the market quickly, as the Iranians try to raise cash rapidly, and will put some pressure on prices, but the aforementioned amount is not sufficient in the grand scheme of the oil market to move it in and of itself, and in any event it is likely the Chinese will buy it en masse at an appropriate discount to market and simply store it themselves, so further limiting general market impact.**

**Although the deal was also formally approved shortly after 14 July by both the EU and the United Nations, the question of what the US would do with it remained in the air for some time.**

For a start, under legislation passed by the US Congress in May, US President Barack Obama would not be able to ease any sanctions on Iran during a 60-day period designated for lawmakers to review the deal, beginning once the finalised deal's full text had been submitted to Congress. In the event that the deal was opposed to the degree that a 'disapproval resolution' was passed, then Obama had the right to veto the resolution, in which case he then needed 34 votes, or more than one-third of the Senate, to sustain the veto. Indeed, there was the distinct possibility that US investors would have remained shackled by the core Iran Sanctions Act until at least the end of 2016, when this specific legislation is set to expire.

In this context, the US Treasury long ago designated Iran's financial sector as a "primary money laundering concern," particularly in connection with the state's alleged financing of terrorism and pursuit of its nuclear programme. In and of itself, this does not preclude banks undertaking transactions with Iran, but it does mean that any bank that has any business in US dollars – all of which are ultimately settled on US soil – would be subject to a range of punitive measures, including custodial and monetary penalties. Even if transactions – including insurance for shipping hydrocarbons, for example – were not conducted in US dollars, then the US Treasury could bring penalties against any and all banking and insurance companies both with subsidiaries in the US or which had other dealings in the US currency.

**Having said that, there were always plenty of firms who would have been willing to engage with the Iranians on both the insurance and banking fronts, despite these caveats, once the 14 July deal had been signed, from Scandinavia through China to India, with the latter two being the most likely.** Indeed, given the lack of concern that both China and India have perennially shown over US sanctions on importing oil directly from Iran itself, it was difficult to believe that banks in either country would be too worried about the US Treasury's banking sanctions, partly because they have less business in the US, partly because they do not believe their own countries would re-impose sanctions on Iran in any event, and partly because, at least in China's case, the US has repeatedly shown (most notably in dealings over China's actions in Tibet and the Senkaku Islands) that it is loath to antagonise China, a nod perhaps to the country's massive holdings of US Treasury bonds.

**The close relationship between China, Russia and Iran has not only been evidenced by the ongoing on-the-ground participation of Chinese and Russian companies in Iran's oil and gas sector, but recently as well by news of the ground-breaking bond arrangements currently being made by China for Iran's return to the international foreign currency bond markets, utilising the renminbi and underwritten by the Chinese directly and indirectly by Russian interests.** Underlining that such close connections will remain going forward was a recent statement from Russian presidential adviser Anton Kobyakov, in Moscow, that after sanctions were lifted on the country, Iran will join the Eurasian economic, political and military bloc, the Shanghai Cooperation Organisation, as a full member (previously it had 'observer' status only), joining Kazakhstan, Kyrgyzstan, Tajikistan and Uzbekistan in the China/Russia-led Eurasian equivalent of the EU and NATO rolled into one.

So, there had been the prospect that any immediate sanctions relief came only from the EU, by just lifting its ban on crude imports – totalling 0.7 mbpd before 2012 – and easing shipping restrictions. Indeed, before Ukraine crisis-related political pressures came to bear, the EU had already lifted sanctions on Iran's biggest tanker firm, National Iranian Tanker Company. In any event, enacting early sanctions relief was going to take at least a month or two from when the deal was signed, so the real effects would not be expected until the end of the following quarter year. In practice, then, after the deal, it was always the case that Iran would struggle to raise output by more than 0.3 mbpd at first, given the lack of investment and expertise and as its buyback contracts would not lure IOCs in straight away.

Nonetheless, **a radical overhauling of the legal architecture of Iranian oil and gas agreements has been in progress in Tehran's corridors of power for some time now, specifically aimed at enticing greater participation from Western oil and gas companies both in increasing output from ageing oil fields and in optimising yields from developing oil and gas fields.** These new contract templates – the 'Integrated Petroleum Contract' (IPC) – designed by the Ministry of Oil will not need approval by the People's House (parliament) as a whole. The IPC is set to have a longer contract period (20 to 25 years), to be extended to include production as well as exploration and development, to have a continuous payment schedule once production has started and to offer full cost recovery, albeit with incentives for cost minimisation. The IOCs will also be able to establish a joint venture agreement with the NIOC or a relevant subsidiary to manage oil and natural gas exploration, development and production projects, along with the possibility to extend into enhanced oil recovery phases. Whilst they will still not have ownership of the reserves, IOCs will also be allowed to help manage the projects and will be paid a share of the project's revenue in instalments once production starts, although the payment terms will be adjustable as the project progresses. Finally, to help facilitate knowledge and technology transfers, which is one of the key upsides from IOC participation as far as Iran is concerned, the IPC will require IOCs to fulfil Iran's local content requirement, which will be 51% of the contract.

**Even ahead of the introduction of these new deal parameters there had been no shortage of interest from Western firms visiting Tehran, with senior executives from many of the top global firms – with the exception of the US, overtly at least – pressing the flesh at the Oil Ministry, including those from Italy, the Netherlands, Austria, France and, in incremental significance, from the UK and Germany.** The nationalities of these emissaries is entirely unremarkable, given the widening political schism between the EU and the US since the revelations by Edward

Snowden of wide-scale spying by US intelligence agencies on senior figures in the governments of Europe, as mentioned.

**The increasing presence of major EU firms in Tehran's corridors of power over the past few months is also likely to undermine the view of those who think that the US Republican Party will inevitably aim to scupper the signing of a long-term deal with Iran, involving the concomitant removal of all sanctions.** Quite aside from the geopolitical importance of Iran in the ongoing fight against Islamic State (IS) in the Middle East – there have been numerous reports of extensive US-Iranian military cooperation against IS – the Republican Party's historical anti-Iranian view over the past 36 years is being undermined further by the fact that it has always been the party of 'big oil'. Indeed, **American IOCs are finding that their ability to leverage the enormous power of their direct and indirect donations to the US parties, especially the Republicans, into a softening stance in the nuclear negotiations has increased exponentially. Consequently the chances of the Republican Party, so close to the next presidential elections in 2016, flying in the face of the desire of the IOCs – their major funders after all – to get back into the scramble for their share of Iran's vast hydrocarbons riches is dramatically decreased. The same applies to the Democratic Party, which receives enormous funding from 'big finance' firms.**

Moreover, given the pattern of power in the Middle East as it currently playing out, **Iran is also vital in allowing US firms to exploit the equally huge resources in neighbouring Iraq.** As it stands, nothing is going to happen in Iraq without the Iranians' say-so, given the power that it wields on the ground in the form of its militias, which extends all the way through its political system.

# Iraq

Iraq's **master plan is to produce 4 mbpd by the end of 2015 and 9 mbpd by 2020,** with much of this being dependent on two long-term factors: a sustained deal with the Kurdistan Regional Government (KRG) and the ongoing and successful development of its giant West Qurna field, located 65 km northwest of the southern port city of Basra, which, with total estimated recoverable reserves of 43 billion barrels (bbl) of oil in place, makes it the second biggest field in the world after Saudi Arabia's Ghawar. This is in addition, of course, to the sustained lower oil price complex that began as Saudi sought to price out the nascent shale energy threat.

However, unlike Ghawar's numbers, and those of many neighbouring countries, **Iraq's reserves figures look solid – in fact if anything an under-estimate – with much verification work done by the Americans when they were on the ground in Iraq, as well as the numbers produced by the international oil companies before, during and after the occupation,** and the Iraqi administration itself. With the current development programme comprising Phase 1 (operated by ExxonMobil, Royal Dutch Shell, Petro China and Iraq's own South Oil Company) holding around 9 bbl reserves and Phase 2 (operated by Lukoil) with about 14 bbl reserves, in theory West Qurna could be a game changer for the global oil market. In practice, though, there remain questions over the degree to which Iraq's ambitious output plans will be realised on schedule, particularly with regard to West Qurna-1 and relations with the KRG.

Iraq Key Cities

Source: CIA World Factbook

In the case of the former, disagreements between the US energy giant and the Iraqi government in Baghdad over the former's dealings with the KRG have served to slow development progress on the field ever since the original contract was signed in 2009. Ultimately this led to ExxonMobil selling 35% of the 60% stake that it held with RDS to the Chinese (25%) and Indonesia's Pertamina (10%) in November 2013, but prior to this Russian oil giant Rosneft was very close to buying out almost the entire stake from Exxon, and it was only when the US government vetoed the idea with Exxon that the company started to look elsewhere. However, given the rapidly changing political dynamics between Russia, Iran and Iraq, there are likely to be opportunities in West Qurna-1 for Russian firms in the near future.

**Iraq: Selected Oil And Gas Infrastructure**

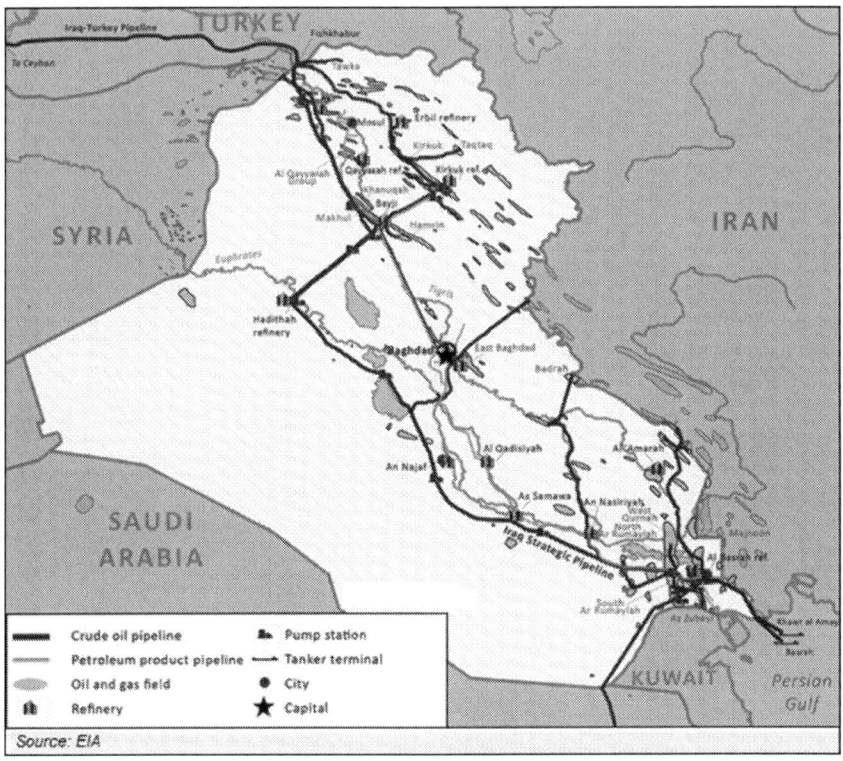

For ExxonMobil the decision to sell the rest of its stake in West Qurna-1 is being made all the more palatable by continued delays in the Common Seawater Supply Facility (CSSF), which would treat seawater from the Gulf and pump it more than 100 km inland for the water-injection purposes required to boost reservoir pressure in both West Qurna phases, but more urgently in the first, more mature, field. In this respect, industry reports stated that the lack of water for injection led to a decline in production at West Qurna-1 in the first half of 2014 of 40% to 300 kbpd from the same period in 2013, and it is unlikely that the CSSF will become fully operational until mid-2018.

Similar delays are apparent as well in the matter of exporting oil from the south. For some time now, the available pumping and storage capacity at the main export depot of Fao has been constrained, both by lower than required storage capacity and by its pumps not being powerful enough. Indeed, the delay in building the 24 new storage tanks envisaged has necessitated the construction, for the new single point mooring systems, of interim pipelines bypassing the terminal. As a consequence, oil is pumped onto tankers directly from more than 100 km onshore and any halt to offshore loading – which can often be weather-related – can force a reduction in production at the West Qurna fields. Until the problems at Fao are addressed, expanded or new pipelines linking the existing offshore terminals at Khor al-Amaya and Al-Basra to onshore facilities will be irrelevant in bringing seaborne export capacity up to the 8 mbpd sufficient to support Iraq's top-end production and export targets for 2020.

In the latter's case, meanwhile, the KRG's Prime Minister, Nechirvan Barzani, has repeatedly warned that if Baghdad does not honour its part of budget cash for oil deal struck in December 2014 then nor will the Kurds. This deal involved the KRG having agreed to export up to 550,000 bbl/d of oil from its own fields and Kirkuk via Iraq's State Oil Marketing Organisation (SOMO), in return for which Baghdad was to have re-instated all budget payments to the Kurds that it had stopped in 2014 as punishment for the semi-autonomous region's moves to export oil independently.

It is not just the money in which the KRG is interested, but rather what it signifies in terms of an acknowledgement of the Kurds' wider involvement in the Iraqi state, in particular its apparent role as the West's 'boots on the ground fighting' proxy – the Peshmerga – against Islamic State (IS). The understanding between the US and the

Kurds was always that if the Kurds held the north, then the KRG's claims to have a completely autonomous state for the Kurds would be expedited. This, though, was not a notion that was necessarily fully shared by Baghdad. The Shiite-dominated Iraqi government and its backers in Iran have sought to prevent the Kurds from consolidating control over the oil-rich province of Kirkuk, and they continued to do so by operating through Shiite militias that were battling alongside the Peshmerga against the Islamic State and playing off the personal ambitions of the Kirkuk governor.

**Iraq's Total Petroleum And Other Liquids Production And Consumption (mbpd)**

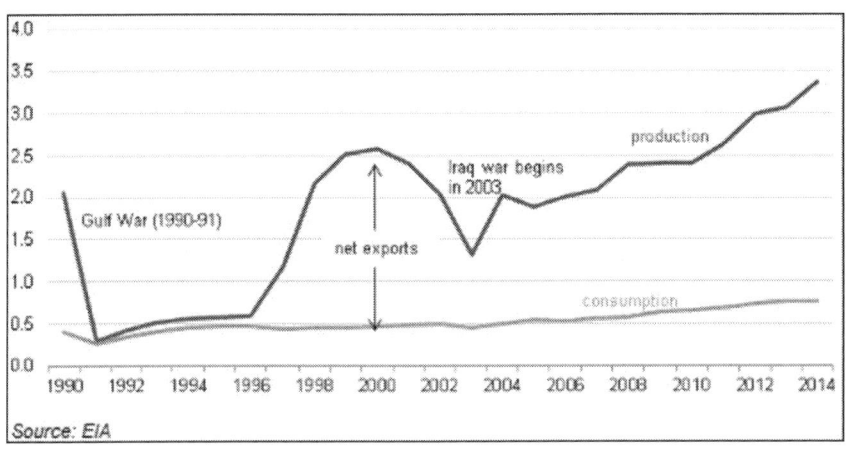

For West Qurna-2 the outlook is far more unequivocally propitious from both a commercial standpoint and from the perspective of broader Moscow-backed geopolitical imperatives. 2014's results for the firm revealed a decline in net income of 39% (to USD4.75 billion), resulting in considerable part from the drop in oil and gas prices, of course, but also significantly negatively impacted by impairments that included dry-hole write-offs of USD794 million on projects in the Ivory Coast, Ghana and Russia itself, as well as a USD761 million charge related to the Tsentralno-Astrakhanskoe gas condensate field in the Volga region. In direct contrast, the 5%

overall rise in oil and gas production for the year was largely a function of additional output from the West Qurna-2 deposit. Even more specifically, the success so far of the West Qurna-2 development means that, by the end of March, Lukoil will have recouped all of the officially stated amount spent in developing the field (USD5 billion), so allowing it to reinvest the funds in expanding output further, as the project is intended to be self-financing.

## Iraq's Monthly Crude Oil Exports By Location 2013-2014 (mbpd)

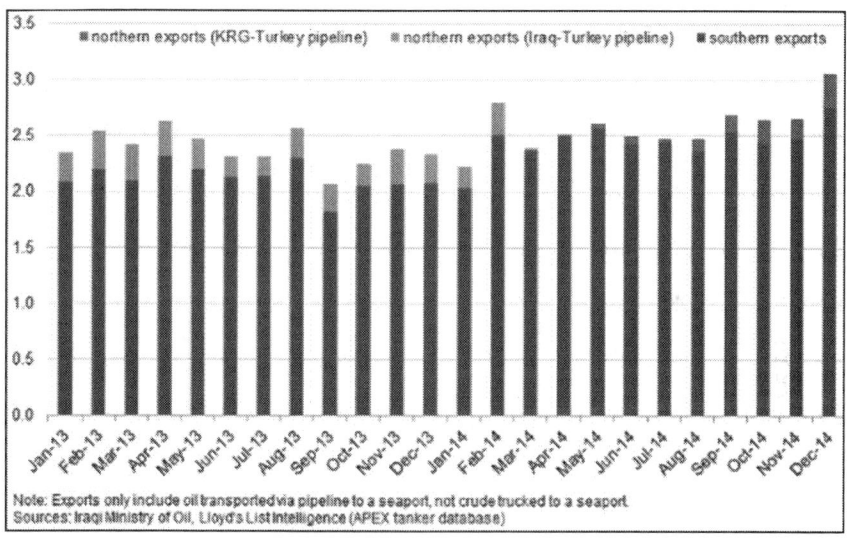

In this respect, this self-financing element kicked in after production surpassed the 120,000 bbl/d minimum point necessary at which it started to receive payback from the Iraqi government at a rate of USD1.15 per barrel (/bbl). Lukoil has seriously upped the ante on boosting current output (around 400,000 bbl/d, compared to 120,000 bbl/d from just the middle of 2014) from the first two phases of the Early Oil Mishrif formation development phase to 550,000 bbl/d by the completion of the second phase of the project (the Mishrif Full Field development). In order to reach this water injection techniques will be utilised, and the Tuba-Fao Project (which provides for the construction of two pipelines, up to 120 km each, between the existing Tuba Tank Farm and the Fao Tank Farm, the main export hub in Iraq located on the of the Persian Gulf coast) will be optimised. Moreover, given that such plans are part of an existing ongoing project, Lukoil is only likely to be minimally affected by the recent news that the Iraqi government has been lobbying for IOCs to postpone new projects and delaying already committed projects, with industry sources saying that the Russians have only offered to postpone USD200 million of investment in total. The next phase of Lukoil's plan to up the output of West Qurna-2 to at least 1.2 mbpd by 2020 (which involves the initiation of full-scale field development of the deeper Yamama formation to add another 650,000 bbl/d) also looks realistic, if the company's current rate of progress on the field is any indication.

# Financial Institutions And Their Great Fix

The **1973 Oil Crisis prompted not only a shift in global geopolitical power, from being decisively located in the West to being dependent in large part on the hydrocarbons output from Middle Eastern producers, but also heralded a shift in those who pulled the levers of financial power, from governments to financial institutions.** The catalyst for this latter shift was simple: following the 1973 Oil Crisis and the re-designing of production contracts between the West and the Middle East (more in the latter's favour), vast quantities of oil money ('petrodollars') flooded into the region. These huge sums in turn – given the relatively underdeveloped state of the Middle East's own financial system – were promptly entrusted back to the West; not though, crucially, in the form of government-controlled investment instruments (such as government bonds), but rather were placed with major financial institutions to invest in any financial instrument that they saw fit (and the merits of which they could sell to the Middle Eastern government officials who handed them over).

As the basis of all true investment is that money will ultimately go to where it is best rewarded given a weighing up of adjunct risks, these financial institutions largely ignored investments in government-controlled markets such as those mentioned above and which generally offer ultra-low risk but ultra-low comparative rewards as well, in favour of higher-risk higher-reward investments, such as equities and foreign exchange (FX). **Moreover, the fact is that these institutions have also built up a massive architecture of oil- and gas-related financial instruments, that is the commodities derivatives markets, which is of enormous significance to the global market in general.**

Unlike those who actually have a need either to lock-in oil and gas prices at some point in the future (retail energy suppliers, for example) or those that require oil and gas for physical delivery (petrochemicals producers, for instance), **financial institutions operate at best only tangentially to the actual business of producing and distributing oil and gas, resulting in extreme magnification of real trends in oil and gas production, or at worst operate at a complete practical variance to the theoretical relationship between production and the prices of certain oil and gas contracts.**

One very effective way of gleaning to what extent a physical market (like oil, wheat or gold) is subject to purely speculative capital flows (rather than actual commercial needs) is to **look at the futures contracts for such commodities (available on the CME website), particularly the 'Open Interest' element of the contracts being bought and sold.** These show the number of contracts that have not been settled to that point in the future as yet and include flows that are entirely speculative in nature.

**Average Daily Open Interest Of Crude Oil Futures On US Exchanges (2000-2014)**

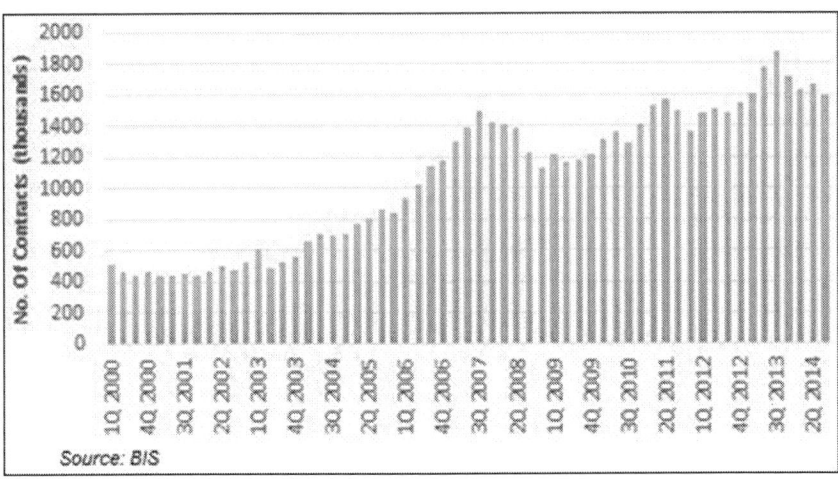

Source: BIS

As can be seen in the chart above, such 'Open Interest' has increased four-fold since the beginning of 2000, powered in large part by speculators buying and selling futures contracts, with no need or desire to hold the underlying physical asset. These numbers have been further boosted by the increasing popularity of 'Exchange Traded Funds' (ETFs) among retail investors in particular who have sought to gain some exposure to global commodities markets in their overall investment portfolios. **This increased interest in holding commodities assets – especially as part of a general ETF – has been in large part reflected in the price action of oil over the past 10 years,** as ETF holders naturally go long of a particular commodity; this powered up the oil price to its all-time high of USD147.27 on 1 July 2008.

Moreover, given that so much of this particular newfound wealth was held on the general balance sheets of global financial institutions, **the oil market has become subject to the ebbs and flows of capital that arise from banks' investments across the board (in equities, FX, government and non-government bonds, commodities, properties and so on). Therefore, investment** correlations arose that bore little resemblance to the fundamentals of the oil and gas sector itself.

**WTI Crude Oil Price 2003-Present (in USD/bbl)**

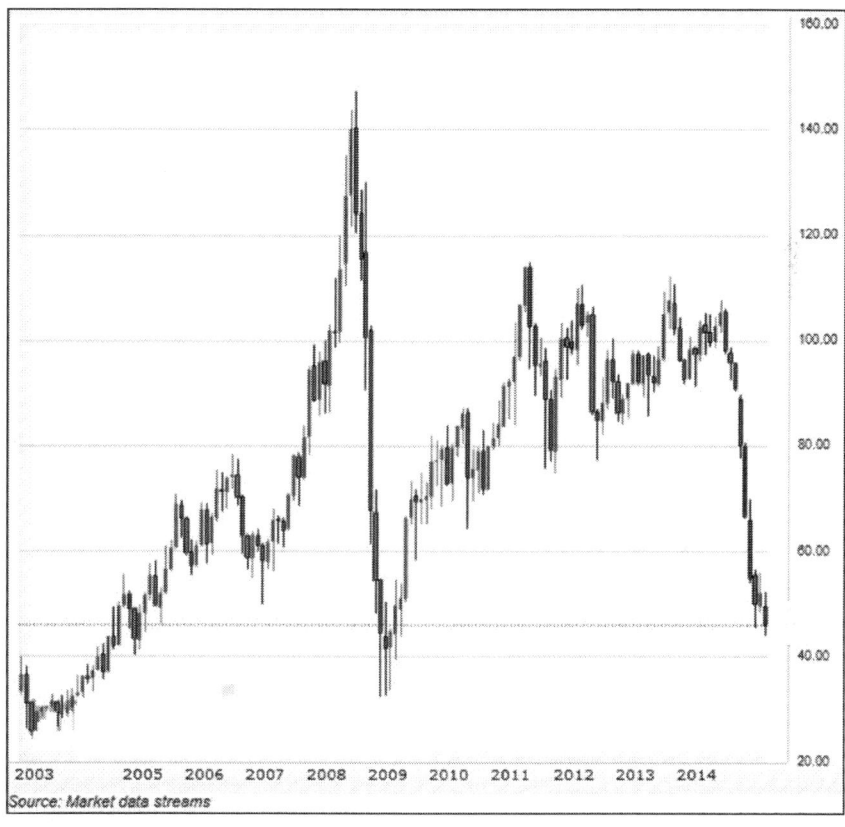

In order to attempt to manage these capital variations, then, **global banks have sought to utilise massive inflows or outflows of capital to try to influence a vast range of markets in general and to focus particularly where possible on those markets which, due to less liquidity, are more subject to having their pricing influenced with less money than might need to be spent in bigger (more liquid) markets.** In this context, it is easy to see which markets have been, and continue to be, most appealing for such influence to be wielded: the yearly turnover of the global equities and commodities markets combined is still much less than the FX market's turnover in one day.

In this context, the global bankers' bank itself – **the Bank of International Settlements (BIS) – recently highlighted that financial flows in and of themselves are in large part to blame for the big oil price movements of the recent past.** The BIS says that the last two comparable oil price declines in 1996 and 2008 were associated with a large drop in consumption and, in 1996, a surge in production. But this time around, changes in supply in demand – which the BIS says have not differed markedly from expectations – fall far short of providing a satisfactory explanation for the sudden collapse in prices. "Rather, the steepness of the price decline and the very large day-to-day price swings are reminiscent of a financial asset," says the BIS, "and, as with other financial assets, movements in the price of oil are driven by changes in expectations about future market conditions."

**U.S Exchange Traded Futures Positions By Money Managers (by 1000s of contracts)**

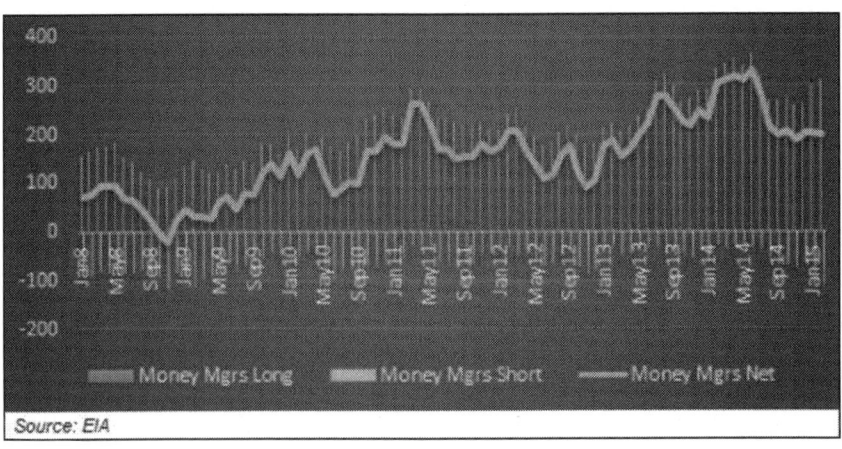

Source: EIA

That **the weight of pure financial institutions' speculative flows has been disproportionately large by comparison with those stemming from 'real-world' demand was further evidenced (at**

**least, by implication) in the dramatic decline of the oil price just before the US Federal Reserve had signalled that it would end the USD3.7 trillion 'Quantitative Easing' (QE) program in Q4 2014, upon which it had first embarked in November 2008.** The theory behind the three waves of QE, of course, was to pump more money – via financial institutions – into the economy to boost economic growth; in practice, though, vast amounts of this increased funding was held on to by the banks, which they then invested into the global financial markets, especially those in which – as highlighted above – they could get the greatest bang for their buck.

So, average daily open interest of crude oil futures peaked in Q3 2013 and declined further after QE ended, to 1.63 million, 1.66 million and 1.59 million in Q1 2014, Q2 2014 and Q3 2014, respectively, while money managers' ETF positions peaked at 330,000 in June 2014 and fell 40% to 199,000 by February 2015. Instead, as highlighted by stock market activity, much of the investor flows that had previously sought to ride the QE waves in the US commodities sector have been re-focussed on the direct QE (or proxy QE) activities in Europe, particularly directed towards key stock markets in the region.

As is obvious, then, **it has never been important in terms of maximising profits whilst minimising risks in trading to know what the correlations in markets are,** both by individual asset, asset class and global geographical variations, which is the subject specifically of the next chapter.

# Trading Oil And Gas Market FX Correlations

There are **three key technical reasons (aside from attitudinal ones, see later *Technical Analysis* section on this) why 90% of retail traders lose all of their trading money within 90 days of commencing dealing in financial markets:**

1. **Inadequate use of risk management techniques** (see later section devoted to this absolutely crucial area of trading), in particular a failure to correctly use stop-loss and take-profit orders at the same time as putting on every single trade they do.

2. **Lack of knowledge and experience in utilising technical analysis** to discern prevailing patterns in financial markets at any given time (see later section on this subject).

3. **Insufficient awareness of the interconnectedness of trading patterns** in different products within asset classes, asset classes in general and different asset classes between various geographical locations are related to each other. This is what this section is about.

# General Risk-On/Risk-Off Trading Paradigm

**Generally, the degree to which the price action of all major financial assets are correlated positively or negatively has varied since this phenomenon fully manifested itself after the collapse of Lehman Brothers in 2008.** Nonetheless, these correlations, which are a function of the risk of systemic failure across the global financial system, remain a significant common price component of all assets in all regions across the world.

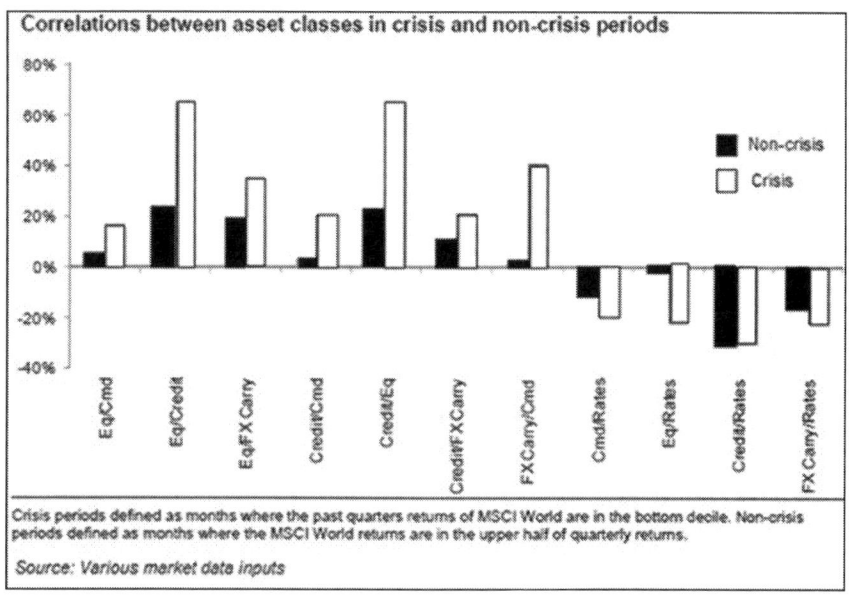

Correlations between asset classes in crisis and non-crisis periods

Crisis periods defined as months where the past quarters returns of MSCI World are in the bottom decile. Non-crisis periods defined as months where the MSCI World returns are in the upper half of quarterly returns.

Source: Various market data inputs

**When the risk of this failure rises there is a shift towards less risk-exposed assets ('risk off') and when it falls there is a move towards more risk-exposed assets ('risk on'); both conditions together being acronymically termed 'RORO'.** Either way, the fact that the prices of apparently disparate individual assets move in tandem (either positively correlated or inversely correlated) means that classical methods of maximising returns whilst minimising risk will remain sidelined for the foreseeable future, calling for shrewder and nimbler investment approaches going forward.

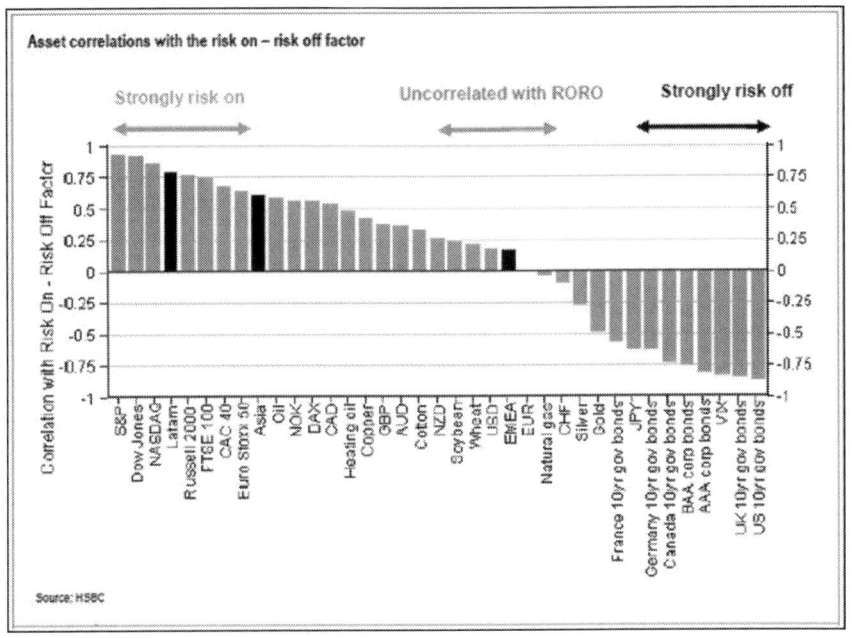

Consequently, in risk-on environments, one might prefer a higher allocation to selected commodities (including oil and gas) that are likely to respond well to increased appetite for risk, instead of holding straight cash (ultra risk-off) or government bonds (where the risk rises according to which country's bonds are held) or related developed market currencies, and then a risk-weighted allocation to exposures such as equities, emerging market currencies and selected commodities if an element of higher risk/higher reward profile is required.

This might be considered a bar-bell approach to risk/return, with the former flight to quality exposures in government bonds being sized to zero in favour of more cash and an appropriately sized allocation to riskier exposures.

This said, the **idea of what may be classed as 'safe-haven' assets or 'risky' ones has changed much in a short time and continues to do so at a fast pace.**

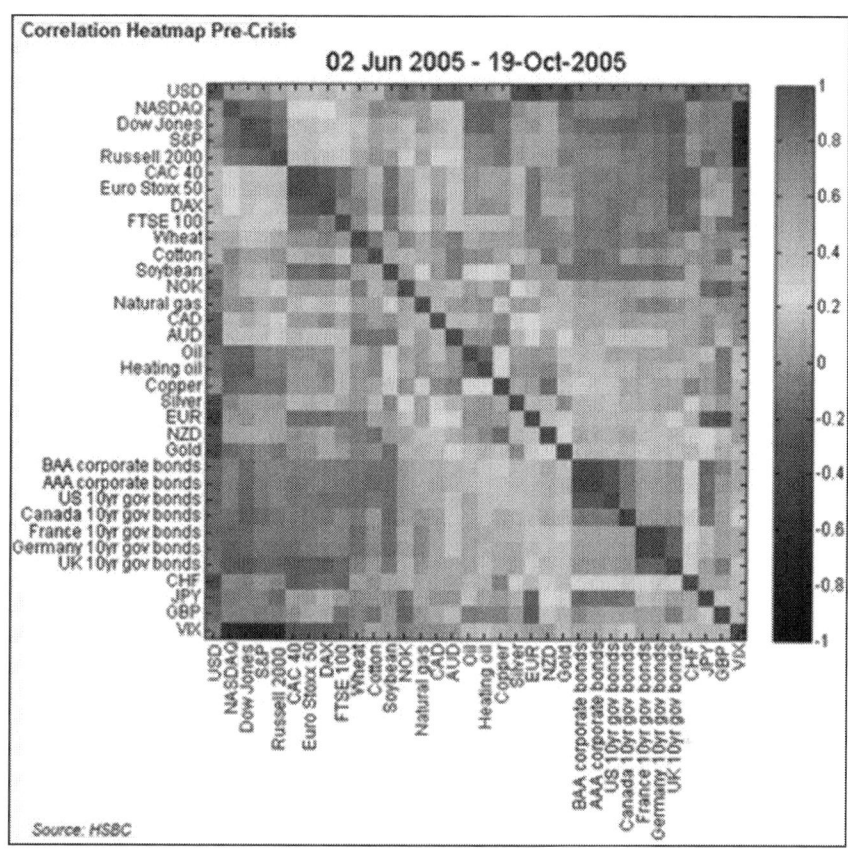

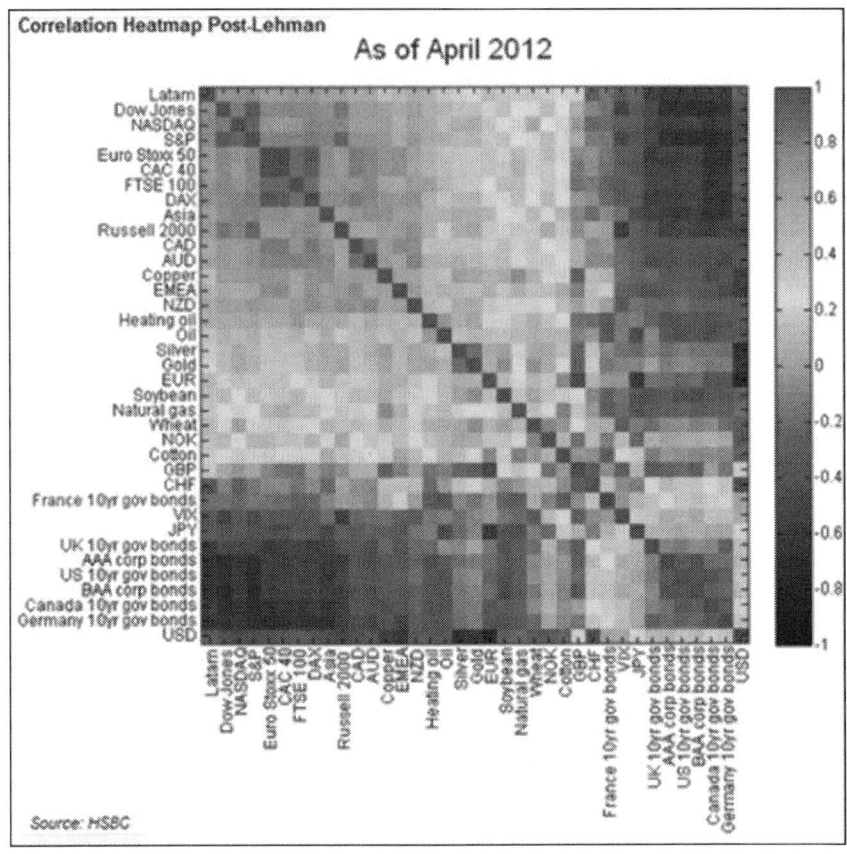

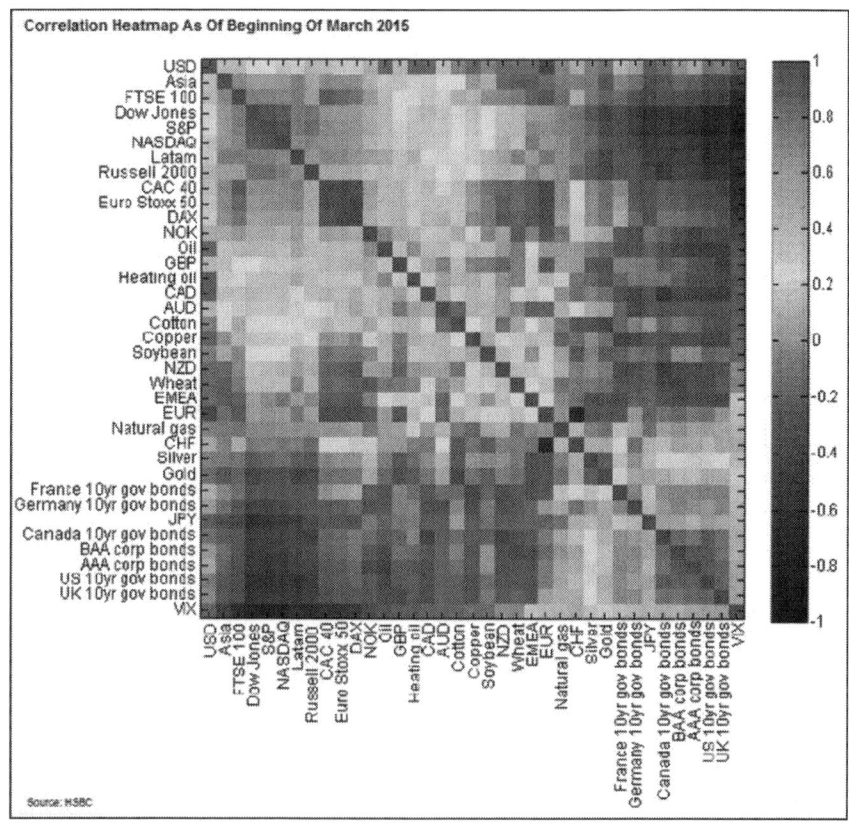

In this context, **it is no coincidence that the global financial markets are experiencing concomitantly the end of the commodity super cycle, the end of the weak dollar era and the rotation away from investment in emerging markets (EM) and towards developed markets (DM), as the dynamics are intertwined and self-reinforcing.**

# Correlation Between The
# Oil Price And The USD

The most obvious – and natural – correlation to note, of course, is between the oil price and the US dollar, as oil is priced in the US currency. **Twenty years ago,** it seemed that there were fairly clear principles for investors to follow with regard to the link between the oil and USD prices: **the higher the crude oil price, the higher the USD (the rationale being that as oil prices rose then the demand for dollars to buy it would increase and thus the USD would strengthen).**

**Over the past 10 years** or so, this relationship has completely broken down, as **rising oil prices have coincided with a broadly weaker dollar, and this has been explained by the idea that rising oil prices lead to deterioration in the US trade deficit (oil and oil products historically represented around 50% of the entire US trade deficit) and thus a negative outlook for the USD and corollary selling of it. The reverse, of course, is equally true, in that a downward trending oil price has coincided with a rising USD.** Although some of this is due to a cessation in the vast number of dollars being released into the US economy (in the three QE programs) and a consequent rebalancing of supply and demand rules in favour of the historical norm, it is also due to the fact that a lower oil price is a huge spur to growth in the US, as it both increases consumer spending and also lowers manufacturing costs (thus, in turn, making exports more competitive in the global market).

Indeed, **it is estimated that every USD10/bbl change in the price of crude oil results in a 25-cent change in the price of a gallon of gasoline, and the American Automobile Association in Washington has stated that for every penny that the national average price of gasoline falls, more than one billion dollars per** year in additional consumer spending is estimated to be freed up.

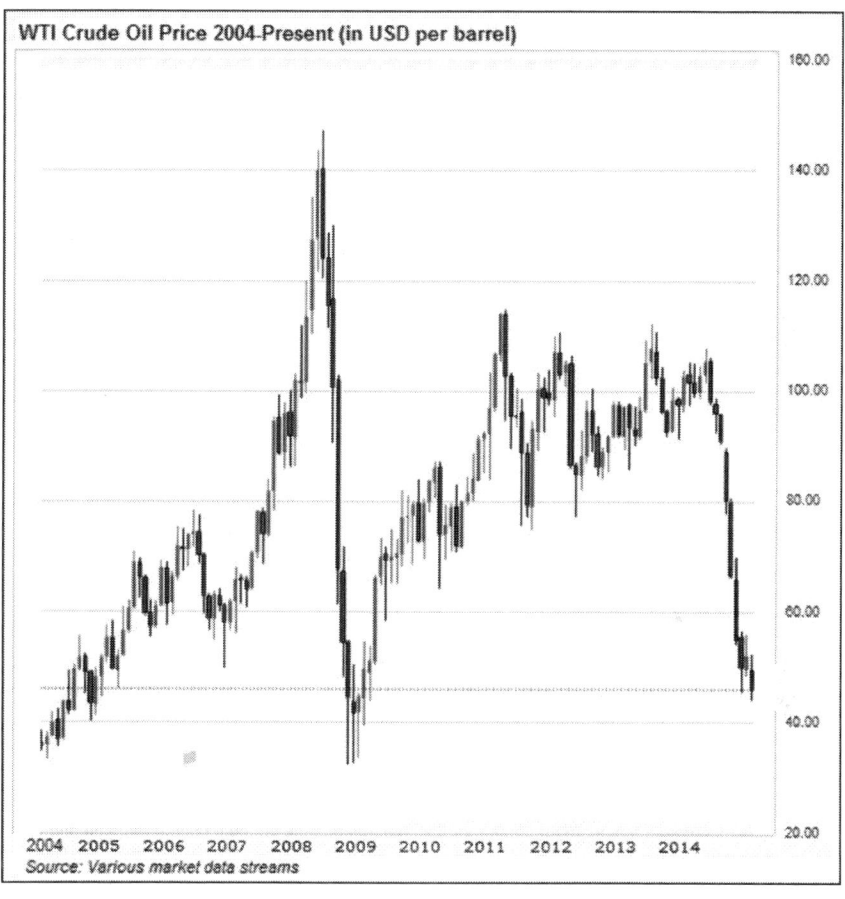

WTI Crude Oil Price 2004-Present (in USD per barrel)

Source: Various market data streams

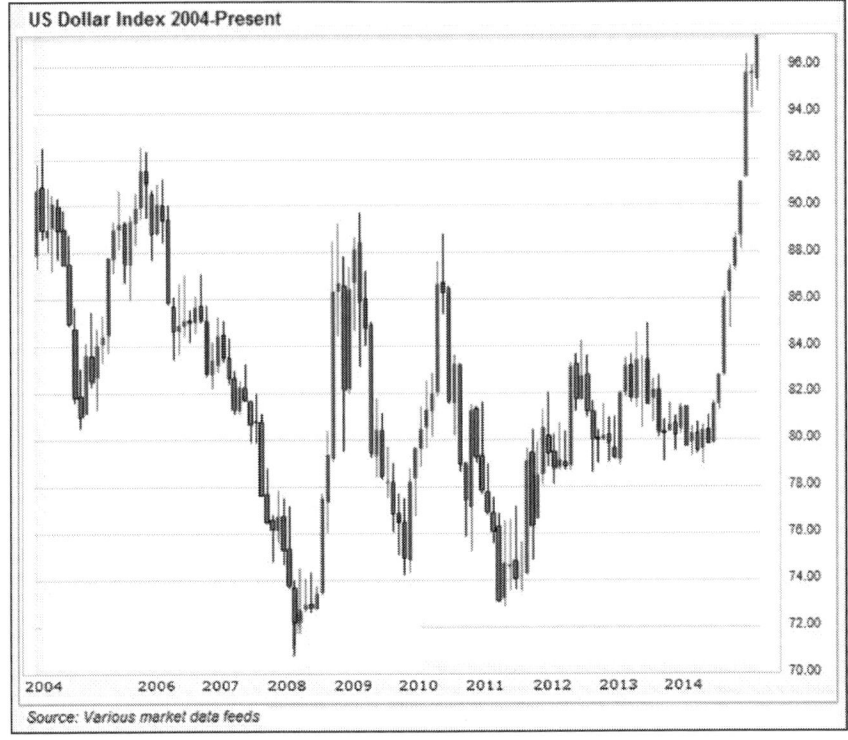

Source: Various market data feeds

**Simply knowing this correlation between the oil price and the value of the US dollar would have netted a trader spectacular gains over the past few months,** and had the trader been doing what he should have been doing on a daily basis (i.e. reading up on all markets from all major sources, watching the key business channels and looking at the trading charts from a technical analysis perspective), then his point of entry for the short oil trade and/or the long USD trade would have been very early on in this major trend change.

### Playing The Latest Saudi Oil Price Fix: Straight Short Oil Trade

Even if he had missed the **slew of announcements from the middle of 2013/beginning of 2014 about the much greater**

**scalability of shale resources than had been imagined before** (in mid-2013, exploration at the edges of the Permian shale and experimentation with new technologies revealed that the aerial acreage of shale was likely double what was initially thought and that much more oil could be squeezed from the shale formations) – shown as Point A and B in the chart below – and the subsequent **announcement by Prince Turki Al Faisal, an influential Saudi Arabian royal and businessman, that the Gulf Kingdom planned to dramatically increase its oil production capacity** (from 12.5 million barrels a day to 15 million barrels a day) by 2020 – shown as Point C in the chart below – there were plenty of other macro-facts that would have provided good entry points for a short oil position to begin with:

1. As mentioned earlier, there were **private meetings between Saudi officials and other senior figures in the global oil industry in New York in October 2014** (which were publically reported shortly after) in which the Saudis appeared to reveal that the Kingdom – far from looking to keep prices high (as had been the normal inclination of OPEC for many years, as mentioned above, in order to boost the prosperity of OPEC member states) – was willing to **tolerate oil prices as low as USD80-USD90/bbl for a period of 1-2 years** (through increasing production), shown as Point D in the chart below.

2. Then, in December 2014, Saudi Oil Minister, Ali Al Naimi, openly stated in an interview on CNN that far from contemplating any cuts in production to support the oil price: **"We are going to continue to produce what we are producing, we are going to continue to welcome additional production if customers come and ask for it."** This is shown as Point E in the chart below.

3. Finally, in the same month **Al Naimi added that Saudi Arabia did not care whether the oil price fell to even as**

**low as USD20/bbl** (shown as Point F in the chart below). His exact words were: "Whether it [oil] goes down to USD20, USD40, USD50, USD60, it is irrelevant." This was unusually straightforward for a Middle Eastern oil minister and as such should have been acted on immediately.

Aside from these huge pointers to going short oil, **technical analysis was also confirming the same position,** breaking through a long-established support level at USD91.50 (shown as Point G in the chart above), and the RSI levels were consistently near overbought levels.

## Brief Explanation Of Support And Resistance Levels And RSI

Although there is a major section devoted to the subject of Technical Analysis later in this book (see *Technical Analysis* section), it is necessary at this point just to cover the basic of support and resistance levels and of the relative strength index (RSI).

**Support levels** are established where the market has overwhelmingly bought the asset (or the base currency in currency trades) in the past, once it has been in a falling trend, and are found **below the current market price**, whilst **resistance levels** are established where the market has overwhelmingly sold the asset (or the base currency in currency trades) in the past, once it has been in a rising trend, and will be found **above the current market price**.

In other words, in chart terms, support levels can be found where selling turns to buying (denoted on candlestick charts, see below, as a red bar turning to green), whilst resistance levels can be found where buying turns to selling (denoted on candlestick stick charts as a green bar turning to red). R1 is the first resistance level and so on, whilst S1 is the first support level, with the current market price indicated as C.

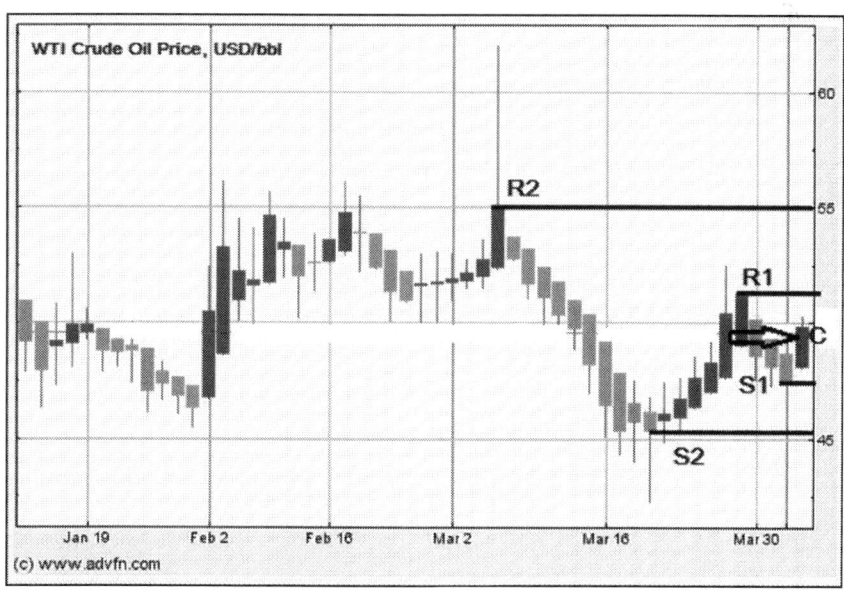

These levels should be the cornerstones of all serious trading activity, as they act (together with other confirmations, as discussed in the *Technical Analysis* section) as signals to buy or sell into a new position or to exit existing ones. It is important to know that the strength of support and resistance levels is increased when additional technical analysis confirmation factors are also present, and one of these is the RSI.

In general terms, the RSI shows the momentum of an asset's trading – in effect, the degree of market participation in its current price movement – and can act as a valuable pre-emptive indicator showing a potential reversal of trend.

For example, even if a pair appears to be rising quickly, if the RSI is showing that negative momentum is occurring then it might be time to look at the other indicators that signalled a long position and look to either exit an existing long or establish a new short.

Conversely, as shown in the chart below, there is a very notable shift upwards in RSI higher before the actual market price follows it.

*[Chart Key:*

*A = RSI rises sharply higher, in advance of the price movement*

*B = Actual market price catches up with bullish momentum on RSI]*

**= RSI confirms upward trend before actual price turns higher**

More specifically, the RSI moves between a scale of 0 to 100, with 100 showing that every participant in the market is buying the base currency of a pair and 0 showing the opposite. **As a rule of thumb, any reading of 70 and above indicates that the pair is overbought, with a possible reversal on the cards, and any reading under 30 showing it is oversold and that the opposite is true.** This, together with the formations of usual double top/bottom patterns, can show up even before they do in the actual price movement ('Divergence').

Similarly, areas of support and resistance show up very clearly on RSI patterns, as shown below.

*[Chart Key:*

*A = RSI shows genuine resistance level in the price, in advance*
*B = Market price subsequently reflects RSI action*
*C = RSI shows genuine support level in the price, in advance*
*D = Market price subsequently reflects RSI action]*

As is evident from the above, RSI's principal use is not in already trending markets, in which it can be used as a confirmation of direction or as an early warning indicator of a change of direction (if above 70 or below 30) but rather in range-bound markets looking for direction.

Here, as shown above, it can act as a proxy for volume interest in particular positions, so that, for example, a sharp spike up in RSI in a market trading around the mid-level could be taken as an early signal of a bullish move and vice-versa.

**Back to playing the latest OPEC (Saudi) oil price fix, then:**

**Trade** = From Point G on the above chart (USD91.50/bbl) there was no announcement, no news, no geopolitical development, no technical analysis rationale whatsoever not to be in a short position and indeed to add to the short incrementally. Therefore:

Stage 1: 'Conservative' (GBP10 per point) **sell order put on as the longstanding 91.50 support level was broken, with a stop loss buy order put on at the same time for the same amount at the first major resistance level (92.25);** this means that the maximum loss on GBP10pp is GBP750 (i.e. 75 pips), with a target of at least 88.05 (i.e. 345 pips), meaning a risk/reward ratio of 4.6X.

Stage 2: **Look for previous key support levels over a longer timeframe of chart** (the above chart is a daily timeframe back two years) to see points at which short should be added to (see chart below, which is a Weekly 5 year+ timeframe).

Stage 3 to Stage 8: Put on further sell orders each at GBP10pp – whilst, crucially, also putting balancing amounts on the stop loss order at 92.25 (as there is no other realistic resistance level beforehand, given that it is an off-the-cliff type of fall) – at the support levels (shown as S2 to S8 in the above chart) that have shown up in the longer-dated chart (the chart immediately above is a Weekly timeframe going back 5+ years). These are at: 88.05, 84.60, 79.55, 72.50, 62.25, 58.95.

Stage 9: Having seen the price bounce up twice from 47.50 and noticed that this was also a major support level back in 2009, take profit on all stop orders, which would be at the 49.25 level, whilst also removing your accrued stop loss order.

**Total Profit for this trade = GBP195,650** (First leg 91.50 – 49.25 = GBP42,250/second leg 88.05 – 49.25 = GBP38,800/third leg 84.60 – 49.25 = GBP35,350/fourth leg 79.55 – 49.25 = GBP30,300/fifth leg 72.50 – 49.25 = GBP23,250/sixth leg 65.25 – 49.25 = GBP16,000/seventh leg 58.95 – 49.25 = GBP9,700)

**It is very important at this point to stress that this trade – and all good trades of the type that are always done by market professionals and which prevent a small percentage of retail traders losing all of their trading money within the first 90 days of commencing trading – is founded upon strict risk management** techniques so, although risk management is dealt with in full in a later section, it is apposite to highlight a few key tenets at this point.

## *Brief Explanation Of Risk/Reward Ratios And Basic Order Management*

**Knowing accurate support and resistance levels is pivotal in determining the risk/reward ratio of a particular trade and in placing orders to capitalise on favourable movements (take-profit orders) or to limit the downside potential of a trade (stop-loss orders).**

Technical Analysis (please see *Technical Analysis* section) is a bit of a self-fulfilling prophecy as whether or not there is any real empirical value in the levels that its classical application produces – the most basic cornerstones being support and resistance levels, as mentioned earlier – the fact that lots of other people believe in it means that these levels take on a trading significance.

One distinct advantage of this collective belief in key levels – exacerbated by their use as triggers for trades in many 'black box' programs run by many investment outfits – is that on a day to day basis, **once a trader has worked out where the key support and resistance levels really are – and this is a pretty straightforward process (see *Technical Analysis* section) – and he has set his risk parameters according to his risk appetite (in the early days of trading to go for at least a 1 to 4 risk/reward ratio) then he should place his stop-loss orders appropriately and stop messing around with his trades** unless something major happens that invalidates the original hypotheses for undertaking the trades in the first place, or – as with the example above – that means that he should add to his position (or scale it back).

More money has been lost by people messing around with their trades or trading through boredom, than has ever been lost in rogue trading operations. **If the trader did all of the other things that he should have done before entering a trade and nothing extraordinary changes – political, economic, technical, Acts of God – then he should relax, and the best way of relaxing in a trade is to put on a stop-loss order and, indeed, a take-profit order, at the same time as putting on every new trade.**

## Net Margin/Trading Requirement (NMR/NTR)

When trading on any platform, **a retail trader will find that his room for manoeuvre in trading is not only limited by the total amount of capital that he has in his trading account but also by the NMR/NTR of that particular platform,** according to the platform's judgement of the risk involved in any particular asset that he is trading.

For example, even if not trading on any leverage at all (instead, trading GBP1 per pip meaning GBP1 gained/lost for each pip gained/lost), a trader will find that for each GBP1 traded the platform will reduce his available account balance by anywhere from

GBP50 to GBP200 or more, depending upon the type of contract entered into (depending on how risky/volatile the platform assesses each contract to be).

Not only will this eat into available investable capital but additionally any losses that a trade occurs as it is ongoing will also be deducted from available capital. So, let us say that a trader has sold WTI Crude Oil at 91.50 at GBP4 per pip. Even before the pair has moved, his capital account will be showing that he is down on available capital by, let us say, by GBP800. If he had available capital before trading of GBP1,000 then he can only afford to have the position go 200 pips against him before he is automatically closed out of the position (and thus wiped out entirely) by the trading platform.

Moreover, it affords no opportunity for hedging positions as they run (see *Risk/Reward Management And Hedging* section). Conversely, of course, if a position makes money from the off then available capital will increase (although this will not affect the amount that the platform has set aside for risk margin).

## Account Size And Setting Targets

In order to have any peace of mind as a trader, **an account with sufficient capital for an individual's trading ambitions is required. Or, conversely, a trader needs to have trading ambitions that are cut according to his capital.** There cannot be an imbalance here.

It is true that, with a GBP500 initial stake in an account, a trader can, in theory – and no doubt it has been done in practice – become a millionaire within five years (see chart below), if one doubles one's money every six months, as the table below illustrates:

| Capital Accumulation Over Six Years From An Initial £500 Investment | |
|---|---|
| Months | Capital |
| 0 | 500 |
| 6 | 1000 |
| 12 | 2000 |
| 18 | 4000 |
| 24 | 8000 |
| 30 | 16000 |
| 36 | 32000 |
| 42 | 64000 |
| 48 | 128000 |
| 54 | 256000 |
| 60 | 512000 |
| 66 | 1024000 |
| 72 | 2048000 |

This, though, requires a high degree of self-discipline, rigorous order management, excellent market knowledge and contacts and highly developed skills of technical analysis.

Whatever the amount of a trader's trading account to begin with, in terms of self-discipline first, he must cut his profit target according to his account balance. A trader should, at minimum, set a risk/reward ratio of 4:1 in the first few years of trading their own account; that is, for every GBP1 he might stand to lose he could make GBP4, based on sensible support and resistance levels.

Concomitant with this, he needs to work out how much is the maximum that he can place on any one trade. Professional bank/fund management traders will typically risk anywhere between 1-2% maximum of their capital on any single trade. Retail traders with no previous professional dealing experience are well advised to risk no more than 1% of their capital on any one trade.

Therefore, a **minimum sensible amount to have in a trading account to begin with is between GBP5,000-10,000.** This allows a trader flexibility in hedging ongoing positions that are not performing well in the very short-term but that he believes (based on empirical evidence) will come good in the slightly longer term. And, of course, the doubling process outlined in the earlier chart is still the same.

In order to make GBP10,000, a trader must make a weekly profit of GBP385 per week over six months. 1% of GBP10,000 is obviously GBP100, which means that this amount must be the trader's stop-loss. At GBP1 per pip that represents a 100 pip movement against the trader that is relatively reasonable in a market of average volatility. As such, it is fairly straightforward and realistic to make the required sum in the target period and even more quickly if using weightings across different asset classes, given proper risk management.

## Straight Averaging Up

Given the idea of optimal trading is to minimise any losses and to maximise any wins, averaging up – if done well – is a good way of achieving the latter.

The basic averaging technique is pretty self-explanatory: it involves **adding to a winning position as the trade continues into profitable territory.** So, for example, in the oil trading chart used earlier, a trader has entered a new position by going short crude oil at 91.50 and has decided to add to the short incrementally as every major support level breaks.

Consequently, with shorts at 91.50, 88.05, 84.60, 79.55, 72.50, 62.25 and 58.95 – all of the same amount (in this case,GBP10pp) – and a stop loss at 92.25, the average level of short is 76.77, with an initial risk/reward ratio of 4.6 on the first part of the trade.

## Layered Averaging Up

Another way of averaging up that tends against the phenomenon of being averaged out of any profit is to **add to a long position on pullbacks to the preferred entry level or the other way around if a net seller.** So, if the trader decides to go short as above then he simply adds GBP1 per pip on any move back towards the 91.50 level, if he is expecting a sustained move downwards over time.

Such tactics are particularly useful if there is an ongoing struggle between two entrenched sides on either side of a trade. A good example of this, aside from the ongoing Saudi/US (shale) battle (which is more complex, as we have alluded to already and will do more of later) was seen in USDJPY, after the new Prime Minister Shinzo Abe came to power at the end of 2012. The Bank of Japan had been buying USD and selling JPY very aggressively in order to support its export market (and thus aid broader economic recovery) from around the USD85.50 level, whilst certain funds – especially hedge funds – were selling USD and buying JPY anywhere above 87.00.

Once Abe had been more firmly ensconced as PM, this battle moved up the values on USDJPY, as the Bank of Japan was given a much broader policy mandate than before. This was in line with those given to the US Fed and the Bank of England, which included looking at employment rates, interest rates and inflation. In this vein, the banks used quantitative easing where necessary together with direct currency intervention and Forward Guidance as a means of manipulating their respective currencies.

It was only when, in fact, the Bank of Japan was tasked with ensuring a broad-based policy strategy – engineering sustained nominal annual economic growth of 3% (there had been no average annual nominal GDP growth for 15 years) and at least a 2% annual inflation rate every year from 2015, as well as commencing a massive domestic bond-buying QE programme (Fed-style) – that the JPY managed sustained depreciation of the sort wanted by Abe and moved through the key USDJPY100 resistance level.

Alternately, **adding smaller amounts to the initial position is also a better way in the minds of many to take advantage of further moves** whilst also limiting the potential for all of one's profits to be eradicated (or even to start making a loss). The converse of this, of course, is averaging down, in which a trader adds to losing positions in the hopes of making money back quicker as the original position reverses but, as mentioned elsewhere, this is a potentially catastrophic idea, and a trader should never chase after losses.

## Value Averaging

As a natural corollary of the above, value averaging is another added value way of managing positions, this time by **constantly readjusting one's risk/reward exposure to a pre-determined level.** Therefore, in practical terms, a trader sets an amount that falls within his risk/reward parameters that he wishes to have in a particular asset over a particular time.

For example, a trader may decide that he wants to have a total exposure per day of GBP100 in EURUSD, at GBP1 per pip. In this event, if the position makes GBP10 in one day then next day he takes the GBP10 out and still has GBP100 riding on the position (at the original price). Conversely, if the position loses GBP10 in one day then the following day he would add another GBP10 at whatever the new price is to compensate.

## Trailing Stops

As a position turns into profit, the amount of Net Margin Requirement (NMR)/Net Trading Requirement (NTR) that a trader has available increases, which can be used either for reinvestment in one of the methods detailed above or can be left where it is, depending on the nature of the market at the time. Nonetheless, depending upon how a position is managed, **there is little point in keeping a stop loss exit order at its original point but rather it should be moved up or down (depending on whether a trader is short or long, respectively) as the profit margin increases.** This is the notion of trailing stops. So, basically, if a position increases profit by 10 pips then move the stop by 10 pips and so on.

**Playing The Latest Saudi Oil Price Fix: Straight Long USD Trade**

**The flipside to the above straight short oil trade, as the correlations showed, is a long USD trade so, if a trader finds that his platform does not allow him to spread bet commodities, then going long the USD would be a perfect proxy. This would be done ideally through going long the USD Index,** established in 1973 (based at 100) as a measure of strength of the US currency against the currencies of six major other currencies: the euro, the Japanese yen, the Canadian dollar, the British pound, the Swedish krona and the Swiss franc. Or, in the absence of the USD Index on a trader's platform, it could be done by going long the USD against other currencies but – and this is vitally important, as discussed in the *Oil And FX* section later) – the currency choices against which this trade should be done need to be very carefully selected.

Very briefly, for example, a number of currencies are heavily influenced by the oil price (such as the CAD, given that it is an oil producer), so this would be an ideal currency to play the idea of a collapse in the oil price. Other currencies, though, the trading parameters of which are defined by non-oil considerations, will not yield such clear oil plays. For example, the GBP has fared generally well over the past couple of years due to specific economic growth projections and to its standing as a country in Europe, but it has not been contaminated by risk fears over the viability of the euro project and has not offered a proxy play on the oil price.

So, the proxy oil short in straight USD terms is a long USD Index position, shown below:

As can be seen above, taking a long USD Index position at exactly the same time as a short oil position could have been taken would have accrued a clear 1700+ pips so, using the same standard incremental position increasing technique employed on the short oil trade, the profits will be of a similar scale.

# Correlations Between Oil
# And Other Currencies

The inverse relationship between the oil price and the value of the USD, then, is clear but the **relationship between oil and other currencies is slightly more nuanced: part of it is a function of the macroeconomic profile of countries whose asset values are defined in significant part by their major role that oil (or other commodities) play in their balance of payments, and part of it is a consequence of the trajectory of the USD.**

In respect of the latter to begin with, the end of the three rounds of QE by the US Federal Reserve has meant that the usual rules of supply and demand have led to a natural strengthening of the USD across the board (as seen in the USD Index chart above), with less dollars in the system and fairly constant demand putting a premium on the US currency. The end of QE and the corollary robustness (to a degree) of the US economy (it has not at least tanked in the absence of extra money being pumped into the system, as yet) has also led to market expectations of a rise in interest rates from the Fed, as part of an overall trend on interest rate tightening, albeit still very limited on the upside. Given that money goes to where it is best rewarded for the concomitant risks involved then, again, the USD has benefited from inflows looking for a relative safe-haven offering some yield(and will continue to do so).

Two years ago in my book *Everything You Need To Know About Making Serious Money Trading The Financial Markets* I predicted the broad-based sustained rise in the USD and also that it marked the beginning of an enduring long-term uptrend, and this view is still intact. Here was the chart from back then:

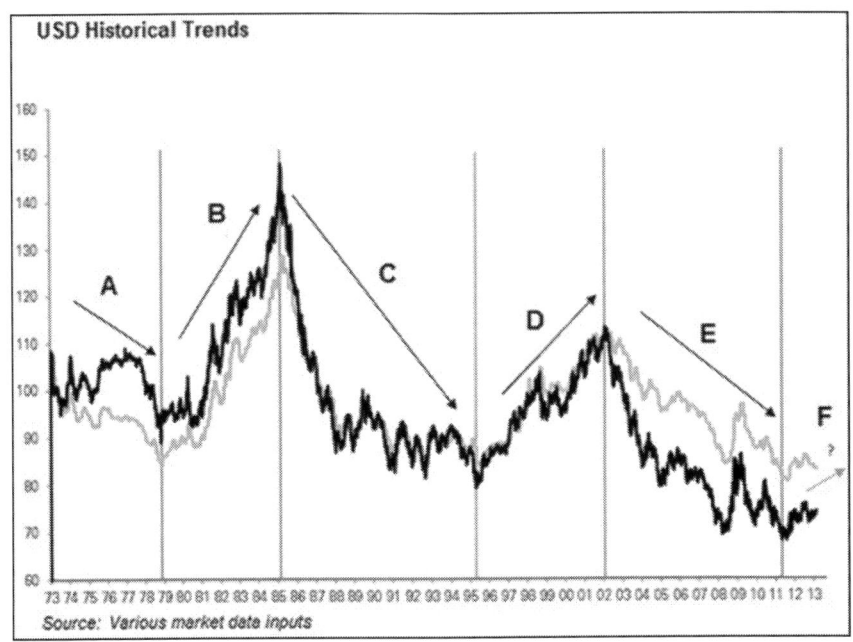

[Chart Key:

*Lines*

*Upper dark black from left to right = Nominal US dollar versus majors*

*Lower light black from left to right = Real broad US dollar*

*Vertical lines = Key trend turning points*

*Arrows From Left To Right*

*A = 6 years, down 18%*

*B = 6 years, up 67%*

*C = 10 years, down 46%*

*D = 7 years, up 43%*

*E = 9 years, down 40%*

*F = Next big trend . . . UP?]*

And here is the chart since then:

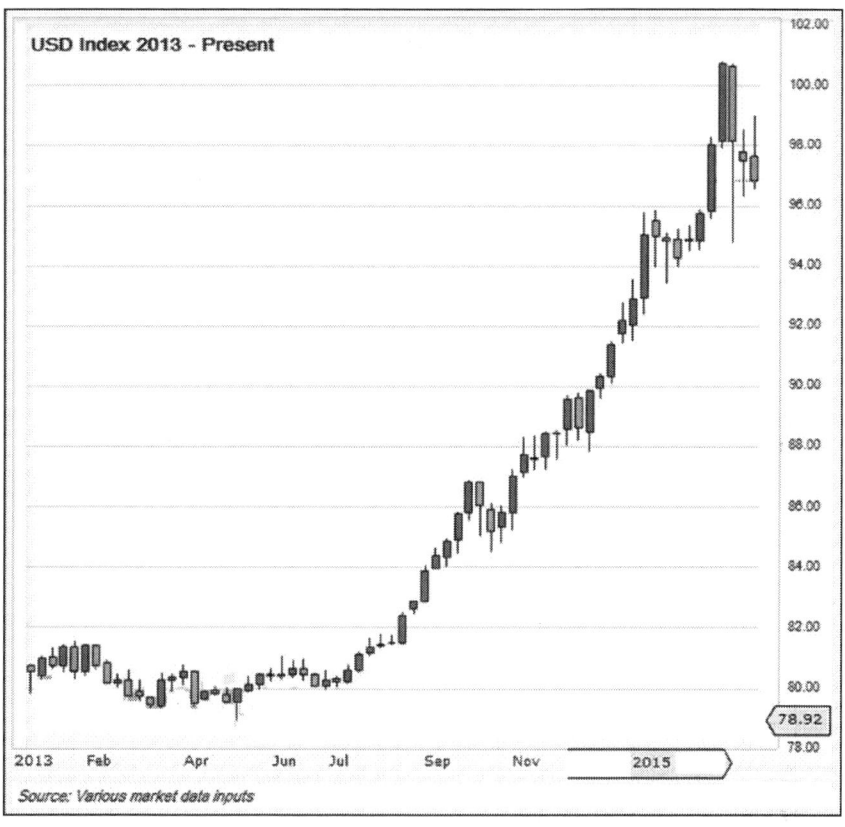

USD Index 2013 - Present

Source: Various market data inputs

## Moving Along The Risk Curve, By Market- And Asset-Type

Whilst, by definition, many currencies in the world have depreciated as the USD has risen, expectations of interest rates rises in the US and the end of QE in the country has also meant a shift in general away from 'riskier' investments, both by asset class and by country. In general terms, **the risk curve moves from least risky asset class to most risky asset class as follows: cash (in a solid currency), bonds (in a solid country), equities (in a solid country), FX (riskier than the previous three categories but extremely liquid) and commodities (riskier than the first three categories and relatively extremely illiquid).** In general terms as well, **the risk curve moves from least risky country type to most risky country**

**type in the following fashion: developed market, emerging market, frontier market.** Consequently, in addition to the decline in oil and the concomitant strengthening of the US dollar, there has been both a move away from emerging markets (and frontier markets) towards developed ones and away from commodities in general to assets with less risky profiles.

To deal with this last point first (stripping out the country-type component) the developed markets of Canada and Australia have notably suffered against the USD, given the significant part that commodities play in the economies of both countries (oil, gold, liquefied petroleum gas and coal being in the top five of Canada's global exports; mineral ores, oil and precious metals being in the top five of Australia's).

To recapitulate, here is the WTI oil chart:

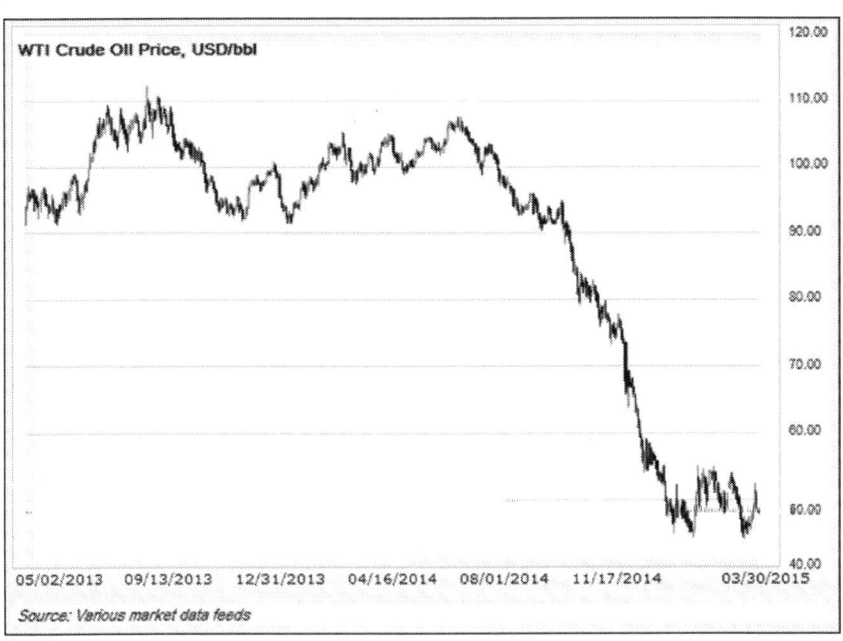

And here are the USDCAD and the USD against the AUD chart (please note here that the USD has been used as the base currency to show more clearly how the AUD has weakened but, of course, in market tradition the AUD is the base currency against the USD).

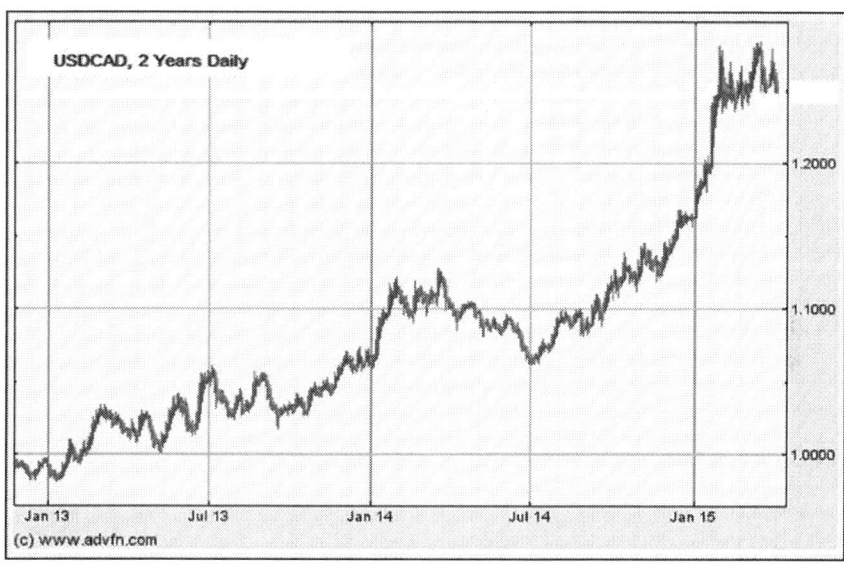

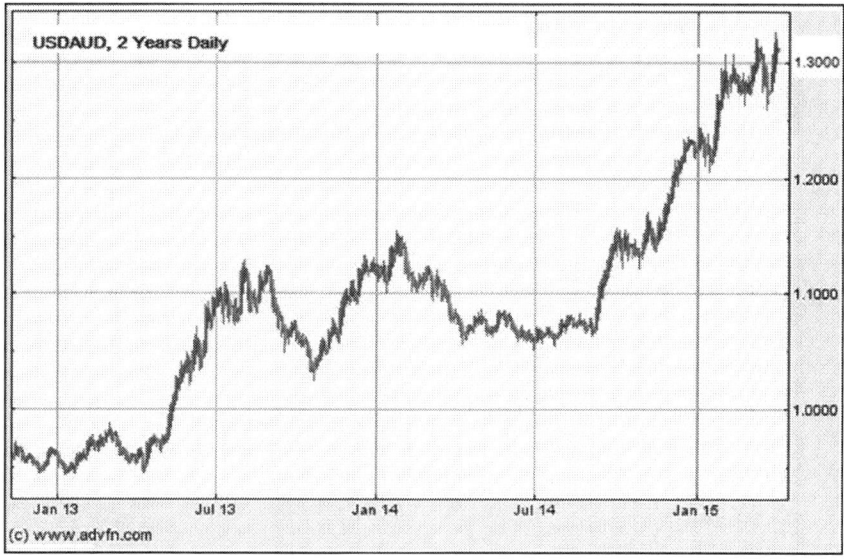

Looking at the first point, this rotation away from buying into EM growth and back towards developed market growth (in particular that

of the US) has also been clearly evidenced in EM currency trends, even those of the once much-vaunted BRIC (Brazil, Russia, India and China) nations, although these are still subject to much regulation (just as well, otherwise they would have fallen even further) and of the almost as previously much-hyped MIST (Mexico, Indonesia, South Korea and Turkey) group of countries.

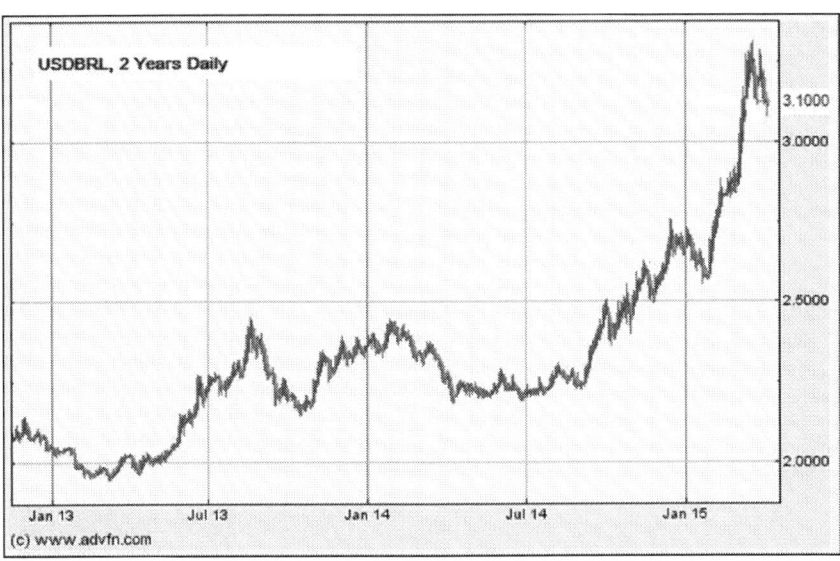

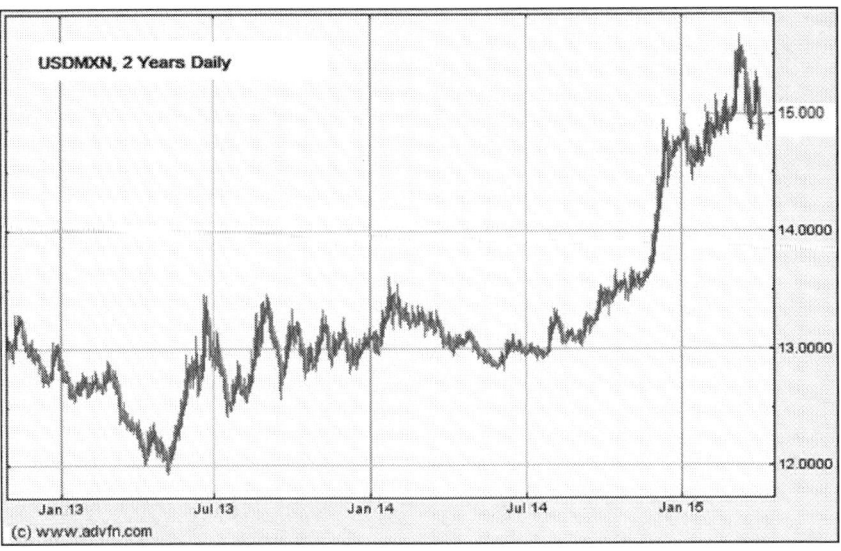

**Risk Rotation Currently Reinforces US Economic Growth**

**This weakening of the currencies of other energy producers and of other emerging markets – particularly those that are major commodities producers (much of South America, for example, notably Chile and Peru) – has a reinforcing effect on this investment paradigm,** as it reduces the costs to the US's manufacturing base, because the price of raw materials falls, making exports more competitive and boosting demand at home, as mentioned above.

To reiterate, though, from the energy perspective to begin with, **it is estimated that every USD10/bbl change in the price of crude oil results in a 25-cent change in the price of a gallon of gasoline, and the American Automobile Association in Washington has stated that for every penny that the national average price of gasoline falls, more than one billion dollars per year in additional consumer spending is estimated to be freed up.**

From the viewpoint of boosting consumer demand, quite aside from cheaper goods being available in shops (electronics that utilise commodities from emerging markets, for instance), demand for the biggest product that most people will buy in their lives – housing – is also inclined to be boosted, as steel and copper costs fall relative to the USD. For example, in an average US house enough copper is used to fill an Olympic-sized swimming pool.

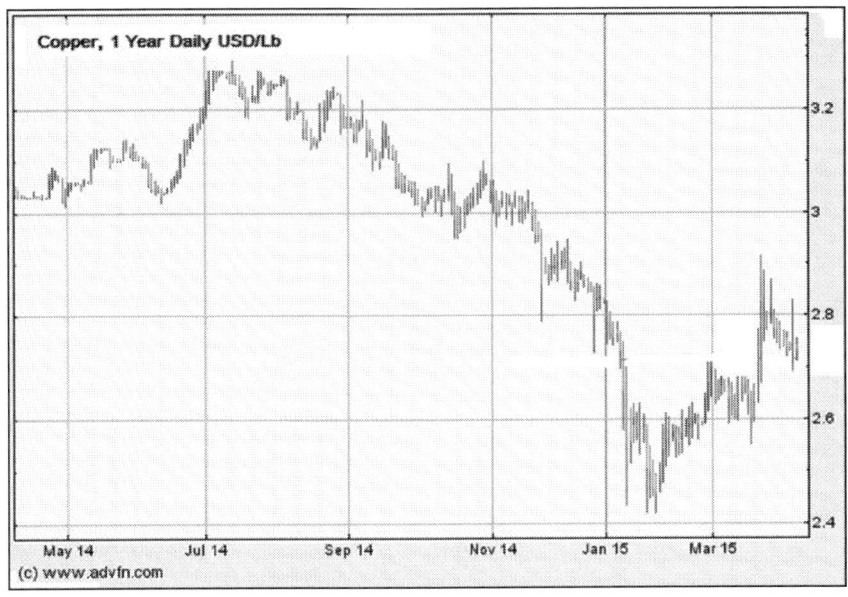

Copper, 1 Year Daily USD/Lb

(c) www.advfn.com

# Cross-Asset Oil And Gas Correlations Trading

There are clearly broad-based macroeconomic correlations according to whether the oil price is going up or down, of course, and these are vital to know in order to effectively trade the corollary assets. To recap briefly on **the current OPEC (Saudi) oil price fix, the intention is to depress the oil price (and adjunct hydrocarbons products) to such a degree that the nascent shale energy industry finds it uneconomic to develop expansionary projects,** by pumping excess amounts of oil over the amounts actually demanded around the globe (see *The Second (Current) Great OPEC (Saudi) Fix* earlier).

However, as has been seen, **although many shale projects have been put on hold, very few indeed have been cancelled outright,** which means that shale energy producers are simply biding their time awaiting higher oil prices. Therefore, in order **to permanently disable this nascent shale energy revolution, it will be necessary for the oil price to remain around the levels seen in the past few months (no higher than USD50-60/bbl) forever.**

The question consequently is: **to what degree can the globe's major oil producers (especially those members of OPEC) continue to function in broader economic terms in this depressed pricing environment,** given how large a part revenue from the hydrocarbons industry contributes to their economies.

As can be seen in the charts below, both the fiscal and budget breakeven oil price for many of the world's top producers are considerably higher than the current price of oil, which means they are looking at fiscal and budget deficits being run for as long as the pricing discrepancy persists.

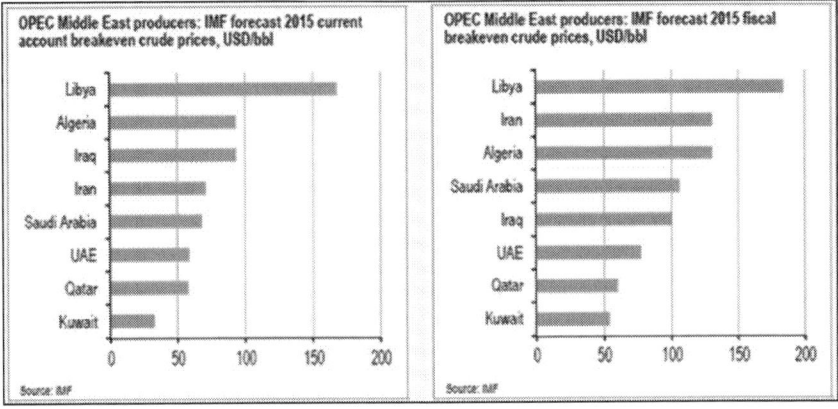

# The US

Certainly, from the side of the US, against which the current destabilising oil price crash strategy is principally aimed, there have already been immediate casualties in the shale oil and gas industry, as we have seen. In sum, according to industry figures **as at the end of the first quarter of 2015, around one third of the 800 oil and gas projects (worth USD500 billion and totalling nearly 60 billion barrels of oil equivalent) scheduled for final investment decisions (FID) this year are 'unconventional', meaning that around USD150 billion of shale projects could be cancelled or postponed.**

Having said this, **the follow-through into US economy in general, far from being negative is actually a net positive.** The political dimension to the US – and, by extension, Western – economic recovery argues for sustained low energy prices, both to boost domestic spending and to keep the price of exports competitively low. Keeping the oil price low is all the more important now, since the announcement in October of the end of the US's quantitative easing programme and the resultant strengthening of the US dollar, both of which would naturally conspire to stymie economic recovery.

Indeed, as can be seen from the chart below, even once QE ended in October 2014, the benchmark US stock index – the Dow Jones Industrial Average (DJIA) – rose at an even sharper rate than when excess funds from QE were being pumped into the US balance sheet and made available for investment in stocks (as much of it was).

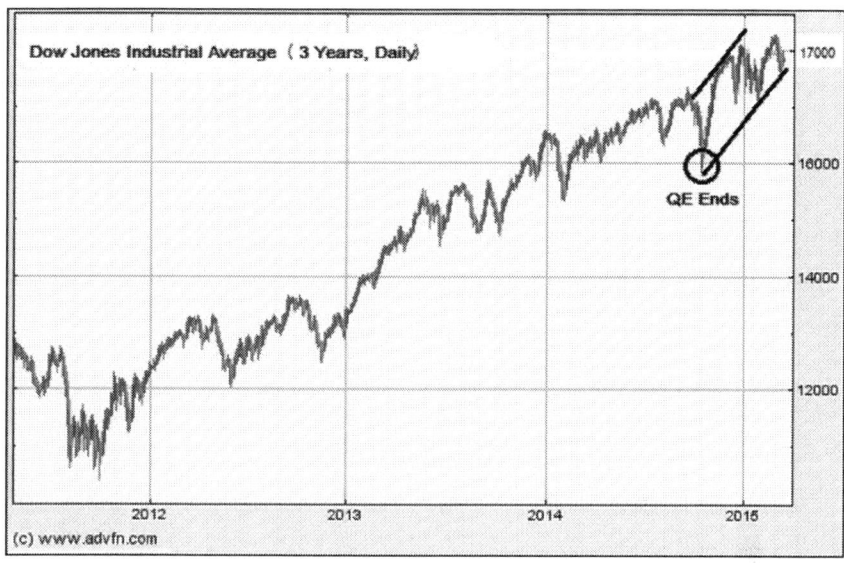

In this context, as flagged earlier, given that it is estimated that every USD10 per barrel change in the price of crude oil results in a 25-cent change in the price of a gallon of gasoline, the American Automobile Association in Washington has highlighted that **for every penny that the national average price of gasoline falls, more than one billion dollars per year in additional consumer spending is estimated to be freed up.**

Moreover, with President Barack Obama's Democrats currently polling low and elections due in November 2016, **it is particularly apposite to notice that although crude oil prices matter to those involved in producing oil or refining oil into products, most Americans and the policymakers who represent and serve them are mainly concerned with the price of gasoline.** In this context, according to the EIA's October 2014 special report 'What Drives US

Gasoline Prices?': "Brent crude oil prices are more important than WTI crude oil prices as a determinant of US gasoline prices in all four regions studied, including the Midwest."

As such, **it is entirely feasible (in line with comments from a number of senior commodities traders) that the US has for some time been constructing a short-term gasoline-led collar on Brent crude oil prices** – selling in the spot market, which has created the current contango market – with a corollary effect on other oil grades, with knock-on effects for the major OPEC producers, including, of course, Saudi Arabia. This would boost domestic consumption in the US, help militate against the strengthening dollar in the export markets and also neatly serve to curtail the basis of Saudi Arabia's political influence in the Middle East, with which the US has grown increasingly uneasy.

Underlining the much closer correlation between the Brent crude oil price and gasoline prices on the one hand and the diverging correlation between the WTI crude oil price and gasoline prices on the other is the fact that unlike the spread between gasoline and Brent, the spread between gasoline and WTI changed significantly when Brent and WTI prices diverged in 2011. From 2000 through 2010, the average annual spread between the US average regular gasoline retail price and the WTI spot price was USD0.87 per gallon. However, from 2011 through 2013, the spread between the price of retail gasoline and WTI crude oil was significantly higher, ranging from USD1.17 to USD1.38 per gallon.

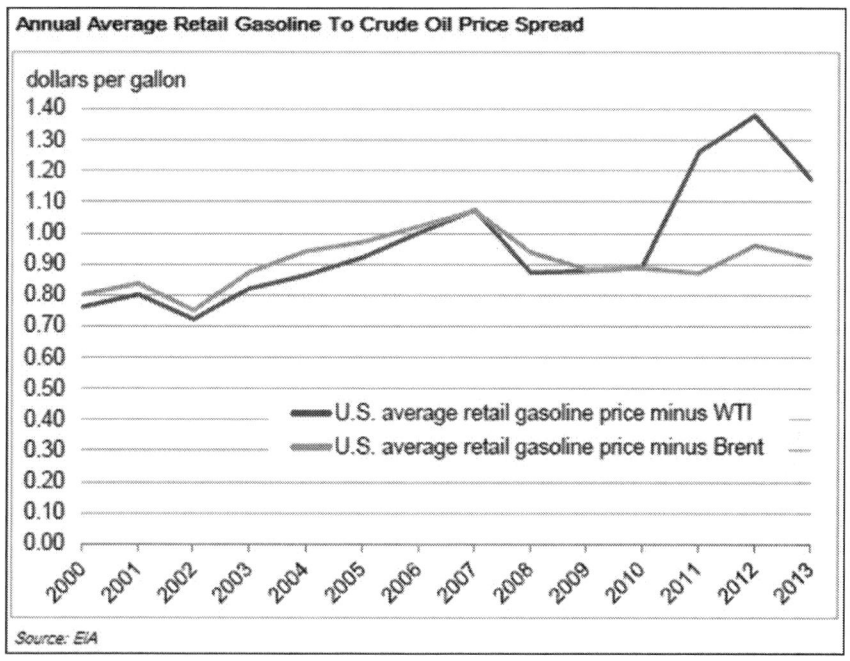

# Canada

Canada is extremely interesting from the trading perspective in that like the US, Canada's manufacturing base and consumption has, of course, benefited from a lower oil price environment but, unlike the US its benchmark stock index – the Toronto Stock Exchange (TSX) – has a much greater proportion of its overall composition made up of companies directly or indirectly negatively exposed to low oil prices than their US counterparts, so the TSX has theoretically been more prone to a downside move than the DJIA.

However, although the TSX has not shown the same level of upside as the DJIA it has not plummeted either, which has been an interesting testament to how it too has benefited from the broad-based lift to its manufacturing base and to its consumer-spending that has come from lower oil prices reducing the costs for its production base, as well as from lower imported goods prices. Moreover, it has further benefited from a broadly stronger USD in that its own exports have become relatively cheaper.

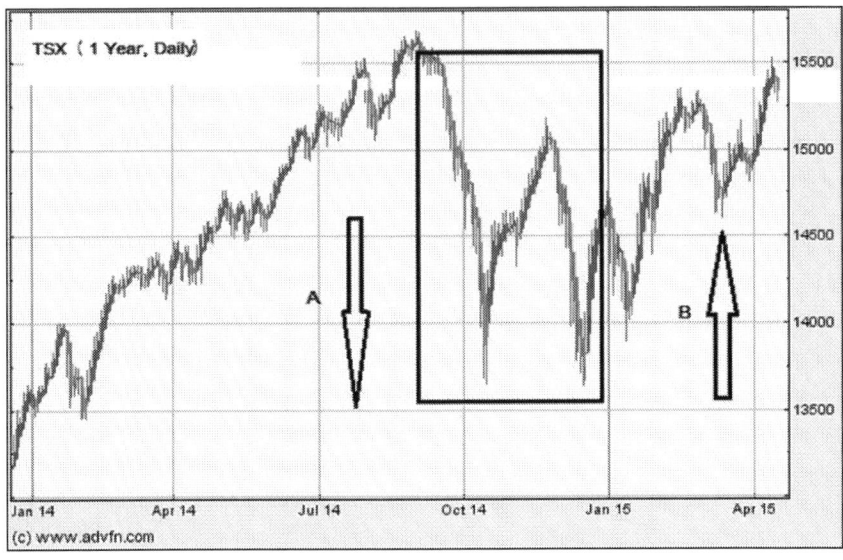

[Chart Key:
*A = Slew of negative announcements regarding the oil price begin from Saudi Arabia*
*B = Broader beneficial economic effects of a lower oil price kick in together with a boost from a lower USD]*

**This disconnect between two key elements of a country's economic profile as exhibited in its principal stock market – and as has happened elsewhere in connection with the oil price (as it is uniquely for some countries both a key cost in manufacturing but also a key part of income) – offers clear hedging and arbitrage possibilities.**

To see this more clearly, it is necessary to superimpose the cumulative returns profile of the TSX and of Brent crude, as seen below.

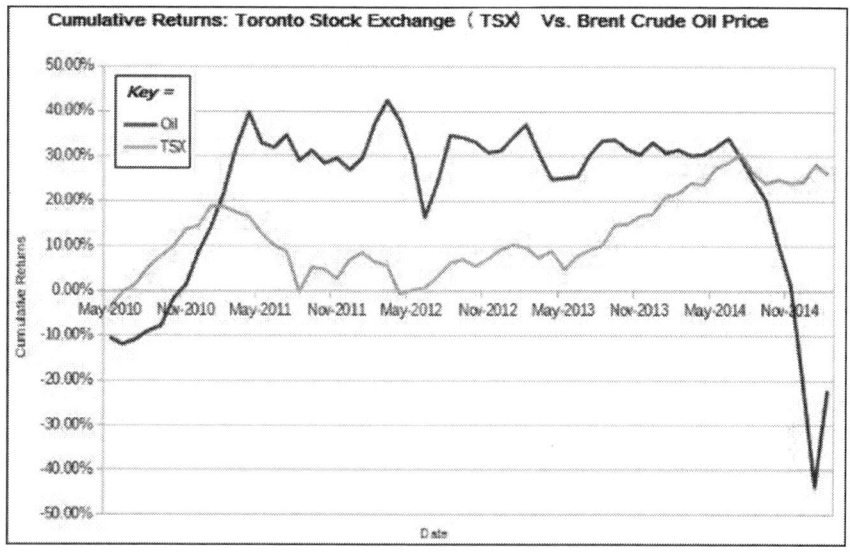

As can be seen above, over the past five years or so the TSX and Brent crude returns have been very closely correlated in trend terms but as of the beginning of the Saudis' negative comments over the oil price direction, the TSX's and Brent crude's cumulative returns directions have markedly diverged, with the TSX having been buoyed up (relative to the Brent price) by the factors mentioned above and by other non-energy sectors performing well.

**Given that the TSX index and oil prices have not diverged to such a degree in quite a long time, but that the TSX has a very heavy weighting of energy stocks, historical correlations would suggest that this relatively recent divergence will narrow over time.** For the longer-term trade, then, this will occur in one of two ways: either oil prices rise with a concomitant increase in returns to match the TSX's or oil prices remain low and the TSX falls accordingly to reflect this. In either event, **the trade with the most likelihood of success, and carrying with it a neat hedging of risk, is to go long oil (either WTI or Brent, although Brent has the wider divergence currently) and short the TSX.**

This is an illustrative example of the way in which such discrepancies between energy-heavy stock markets (see above) and the oil price can be utilised to generate alpha returns with very little inherent risk having to be dealt with through further risk management strategies.

# OPEC Member States

In direct contrast to the effect on North America is the effect on those economies that are extremely highly correlated to hydrocarbons prices, in particular those of the Middle East. **When thinking about the potential scope for oil-driven local economic damage, the size of the local energy sector – without regard for the destination of that production – is an important metric, and oil accounts for around 50% for some of the Gulf States: Kuwait, Saudi Arabia and Iraq** (see chart below).

A simple back of the envelope calculation that directly translates a decline in oil prices into a proportional decline in GDP suggests that, **given a 60% decline in oil prices (which is roughly the size of the decline in front-month WTI crude oil over the last six months), nominal GDP in Kuwait and Saudi Arabia, for example, would decline by more than 25%, which is greater than the damage experienced in 2008/09.** As an adjunct to this, every USD10/bbl drop in the oil price shaves 3.4% and 4.2% of gross domestic product (GDP) off fiscal and current account balances, respectively, in the Gulf Cooperation Council (GCC) economy as a whole. As such, it is forecast the Gulf region will suffer from aggregate twin deficits; -8.4% of GDP on the fiscal side and -3% of GDP on the external side. Consequently, the emphasis in the recent 2015 Saudi budget statement on the funding of projects already suggests that new ventures could be delayed, adding to already tightening liquidity across the GCC. Indeed, with the increased fiscal pressure of a prolonged oil price slump, it can be expected that capital expenditures will bear the brunt of the adjustment, as per historical experience.

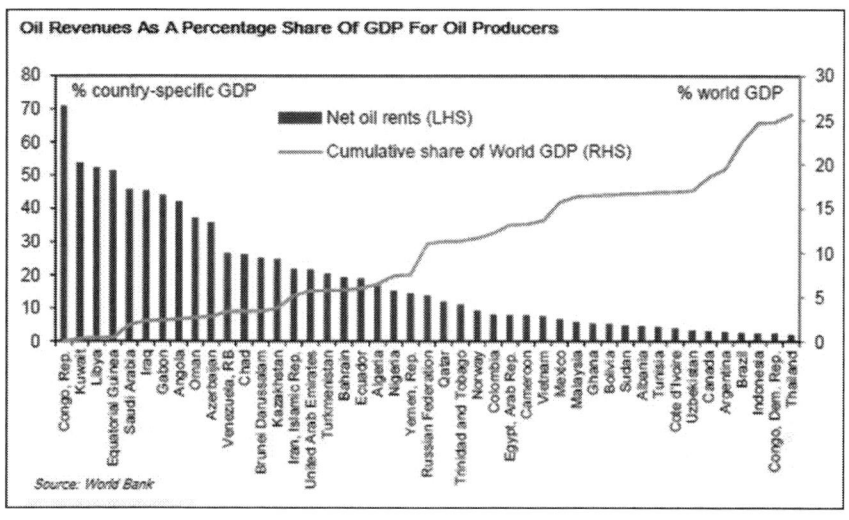

For the key driver behind this war on shale – Saudi Arabia – the stakes then are high, in purely economic terms, but – when factoring in geo-political concerns in the Kingdom – could, in fact, hardly be higher. Certainly, Saudi Arabia is equipped with sufficient government assets to weather the budget deficits that would result from Brent at USD83/bbl for a period of 7-8 years, assuming no changes to nominal spending. Indeed, it has a huge foreign currency reserves war chest (USD745 billion as at end-2014) with which to service a fiscal deficit for an extended period if necessary.

**Brent Oil Prices Required To Meet Various Fiscal Sustainability Thresholds ( US$/bbl)**

| | GS primary deficit breakeven (2015E production) | Debt / GDP | Price needed to keep Debt/GDP constant | | Price needed to reach 40% Debt/GDP ratio in 3 years | Reserves / Public Debt |
|---|---|---|---|---|---|---|
| | | | After 1 year | After 2 years | | |
| Kuwait | $60 | 11% | $63 | $69 | $64 | 102.2 |
| UAE | $64 | 12% | $71 | $86 | $38 | 17.0 |
| Qatar | $68 | 35% | $71 | $80 | $77 | 3.0 |
| Saudi | $83 | 3% | $85 | $88 | $79 | 35.8 |
| Russia | $101 | 10% | $104 | $108 | $92 | 2.9 |
| Algeria | $106 | 9% | $108 | $109 | $92 | 14.1 |
| Angola | $117 | 39% | $128 | $145 | $142 | 1.9 |
| Iraq | $126 | 31% | $131 | $136 | $133 | 1.3 |
| Iran | $133 | 11% | $139 | $141 | $98 | 3.3 |
| Nigeria | $144 | 10% | $158 | $182 | $129 | 6.6 |
| Libya | $185 | 5% | $204 | $230 | $180 | |

\* Reserves include SWF where applicable. Total production includes crude, NGLs and nonconventional oils.

Source: IEA, IMF, World Bank, African Development Bank, Goldman Sachs

However, the notion of doing this will not be universally popular amongst the senior figures in the country who worry that re-building reserves levels may be extremely difficult in the future, given the likelihood of a permanently reduced hydrocarbons pricing complex going forward. Such concerns have been exacerbated by the recent death of the shrewd politically-aware King Abdullah, replaced by the apparently dithering and frail King Salman, which has caused **uncertainty amongst the tribes as to the long-term future of the House of Saud** and their place in it. Notably in this respect, for example, a key figure in the country, Prince Alwaleed bin Talal, who is the Middle East's wealthiest individual investor, has repeatedly been an outspoken critic of Saudi Oil Minister Ali Al Naimi's no holds barred plan to put the brakes on any oil shale revolution, which he has said could have catastrophic long-term consequences for the Saudi economy. This appears to be a view shared by major ratings agency **Standard And Poor's (S&P), which in the middle of February downgraded the outlook on Saudi Arabia's key foreign currency AA- rating from 'stable' to 'negative'. This is hardly likely to help the benchmark Tadawul All Share Index** (TASI), despite perennial talk of it being opened up to direct foreign non-Gulf investment participation.

*[Chart Key:*
*A = Increased talk of market opening up to foreign investors lifts valuations*
*B = Reiteration of commitment to low oil price policy and negative fiscal and budget projections weigh on TASI*
*C = Oil price holds above US40/bbl and then breaks through USD50/bbl]*

The ramifications of the oil price decline on other Middle Eastern countries have varied, both according to their budget and fiscal breakeven price for oil and on the overall balance inherent in their hydrocarbons sector. **One country that has fared better than many others in the region is the emirate of Qatar, which ranks as the world's 'swing' producer of liquefied natural gas (LNG) in the same sort of way as Saudi Arabia does for oil.** This was highlighted in the report released by S&P in which, at the same time as the agency was downgrading the outlook on Saudi Arabia, it maintained Qatar's AA rating with a 'stable' outlook, despite the fact that – along with Saudi Arabia and Abu Dhabi – hydrocarbons account for up to 90% of its fiscal revenues as well.

The key reason for this is the fact that Qatar has a dominant global position in the LNG market, being the largest exporter as of 2013 and having the third largest proven reserves – it has an annual output capacity of 77 million tonnes and raw gas reserves totalling around 872 Tcf (it can continue to extract gas for at least another 156 years at current production rates). Additionally, natural gas prices began to decouple from oil prices in 2008-2009. Finally, natural gas is enjoying increasing popularity over other fossil fuels due its lower carbon emissions.

There are caveats, of course, in that Qatar needs to continue to strengthen its macro-fiscal capabilities, particularly in three core areas: first, by accelerating the deepening of capital markets and sources of funding; second, by expanding the government's revenue base; and third, by managing government expenditure efficiently. However, these measures will help to achieve the desired AAA credit rating over time, and anticipation of a rising trend in credit ratings will underpin gains in the benchmark Qatar Stock Exchange (QSE).

| Moody's | | S&P | | Fitch | | |
|---|---|---|---|---|---|---|
| Long-term | Short-term | Long-term | Short-term | Long-term | Short-term | |
| Aaa | | AAA | | AAA | | Prime |
| Aa1 | | AA+ | A-1+ | AA+ | F1+ | |
| Aa2 | P-1 | AA | | AA | | High grade |
| Aa3 | | AA- | | AA- | | |
| A1 | | A+ | A-1 | A+ | F1 | |
| A2 | | A | | A | | Upper medium grade |
| A3 | P-2 | A- | A-2 | A- | F2 | |
| Baa1 | | BBB+ | | BBB+ | | |
| Baa2 | P-3 | BBB | A-3 | BBB | F3 | Lower medium grade |
| Baa3 | | BBB- | | BBB- | | |
| Ba1 | | BB+ | | BB+ | | Non-investment grade speculative |
| Ba2 | | BB | | BB | | |
| Ba3 | | BB- | B | BB- | B | |
| B1 | | B+ | | B+ | | |
| B2 | | B | | B | | Highly speculative |
| B3 | | B- | | B- | | |
| Caa1 | Not prime | CCC+ | | | | Substantial risks |
| Caa2 | | CCC | | | | Extremely speculative |
| Caa3 | | CCC- | C | CCC | C | In default with little prospect for recovery |
| Ca | | CC | | | | |
| | | C | | | | |
| C | | D | / | DDD | / | In default |
| / | | | | DD | | |

**It is not just an upgrade (or expectations of one) that serves to support equities asset valuations over time but also de facto upgrades in the way in which a market is regarded along the risk curve; running from frontier (highest perceived risk) through emerging to developed (lowest perceived risk).** In this respect as well, Qatar's stock market has broadly benefited from news in May last year that Morgan Stanley Capital International (MSCI) was re-classifying the emirate's benchmark index (along with the UAE's) in its Emerging Markets Index to 'emerging market' from 'frontier market', with a 0.45% MSCI EM weighting. The expectation of this and its realisation led to an upwards spike in prices and investment volumes into the QSE and the UAE's stock markets, as can be seen below.

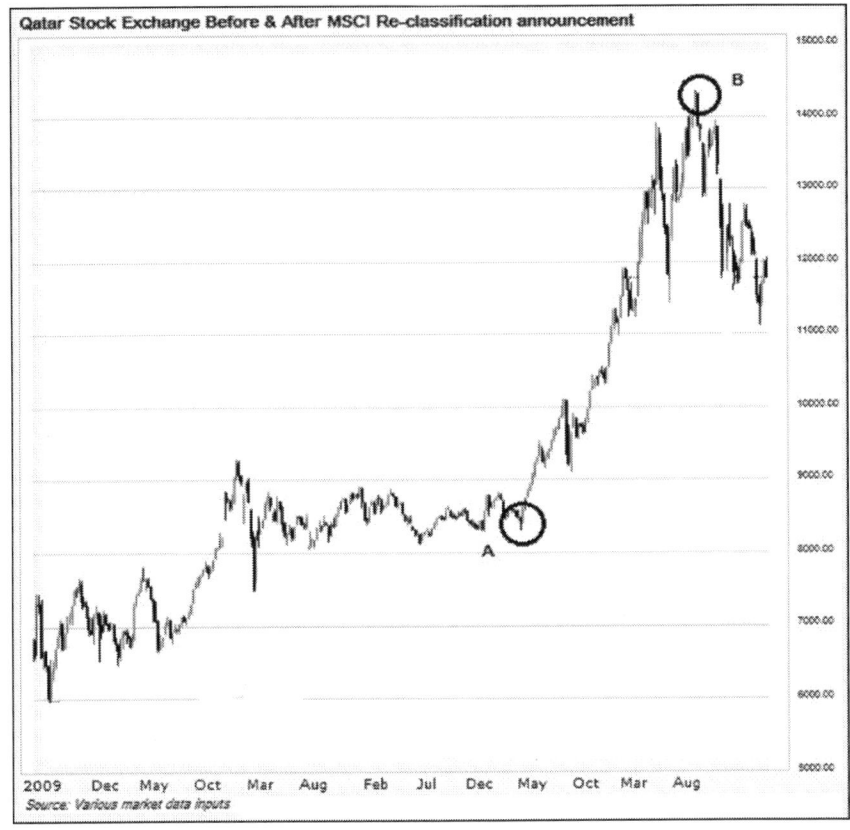

Qatar Stock Exchange Before & After MSCI Re-classification announcement

[Chart Key:

*A = Announcement of reclassification of Qatar as 'emerging market' the next year, from 'frontier market'*

*B = Initial new investment flows hit the ceiling of a lower oil pricing complex ]*

# Emerging Markets

As touched on earlier, **the global financial markets are experiencing concomitantly the end of the commodity super cycle, the end of the weak dollar era and the rotation away from investment in emerging markets and towards developed markets, as the dynamics are intertwined and self-reinforcing.**

Whilst it is true that emerging markets countries (see chart below) have been adversely affected by the aforementioned switch of capital on a global basis, **the degree to which depends on two factors: first, their dependence on the oil price as a portion of their overall economic revenues; and second, the soundness of their economic systems as a whole and where they fit into the overall business cycle of a country.**

**Global Emerging Markets, By Different Organisation Rating**

| Country | IMF | FTSE | MSCI | S&P | Dow Jones |
|---|---|---|---|---|---|
| Argentina | ✓ | | | | |
| Brazil | ✓ | ✓ | ✓ | ✓ | ✓ |
| Bulgaria | ✓ | | | | |
| Chile | ✓ | ✓ | ✓ | ✓ | ✓ |
| People's Republic of China | ✓ | ✓ | ✓ | ✓ | ✓ |
| Colombia | ✓ | ✓ | ✓ | ✓ | ✓ |
| Czech Republic | | ✓ | ✓ | ✓ | ✓ |
| Egypt | | ✓ | ✓ | ✓ | ✓ |
| Estonia | ✓ | | | | |
| Greece | | | ✓ | ✓ | ✓ |
| Hungary | ✓ | ✓ | ✓ | ✓ | ✓ |
| India | ✓ | ✓ | ✓ | ✓ | ✓ |
| Indonesia | ✓ | ✓ | ✓ | ✓ | ✓ |
| Latvia | ✓ | | | | |
| Lithuania | ✓ | | | | |
| Malaysia | ✓ | ✓ | ✓ | ✓ | ✓ |
| Mexico | ✓ | ✓ | ✓ | ✓ | ✓ |
| Morocco | | ✓ | | ✓ | ✓ |
| Pakistan | ✓ | ✓ | | | |
| Peru | ✓ | ✓ | ✓ | ✓ | ✓ |
| Philippines | ✓ | ✓ | ✓ | ✓ | ✓ |
| Poland | ✓ | ✓ | ✓ | ✓ | ✓ |
| Qatar | | | ✓ | | ✓ |
| Romania | ✓ | | | | |
| Russia | ✓ | ✓ | ✓ | ✓ | ✓ |
| South Africa | ✓ | ✓ | ✓ | ✓ | ✓ |
| South Korea | | | ✓ | | |
| Taiwan | | ✓ | ✓ | ✓ | ✓ |
| Thailand | ✓ | ✓ | ✓ | ✓ | ✓ |
| Turkey | ✓ | ✓ | ✓ | ✓ | ✓ |
| Ukraine | ✓ | | | | |
| United Arab Emirates | | ✓ | ✓ | | ✓ |
| Venezuela | ✓ | | | | |

*Source: Various*

A look at the hydrocarbons revenue as a percentage of overall budget and fiscal revenues identifies some obvious apparent winners and losers in the EM sphere, running from left to right of the chart below.

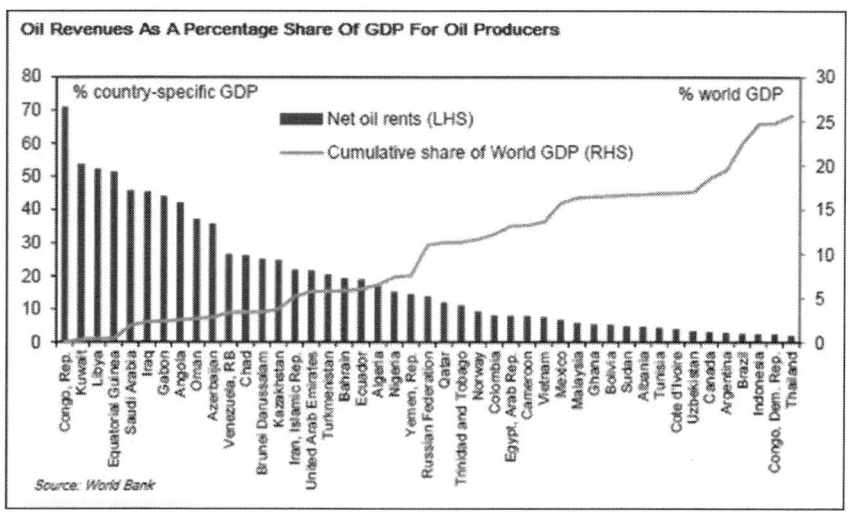

Judging solely on the basis of oil revenues as a percentage share of GDP for oil producers, it would appear that Venezuela is most correlated to the fall in oil prices and is thus most adversely affected as an investment proposition, followed by the UAE (see above analysis), Russia (see above analysis), Qatar (see above analysis), Colombia, Egypt, Mexico, Malaysia, Argentina, Brazil, Indonesia and Thailand. However, **a more nuanced approach is required for weighing up investment in the current market conditions in whatever market it is – either by region or asset class – using RORO-delineated parameters factoring in a lower oil price constant.** The key is to follow what is going on all the time across all key developed and emerging markets every day and to know inside and out what is happening on the fundamentals side of the countries involved.

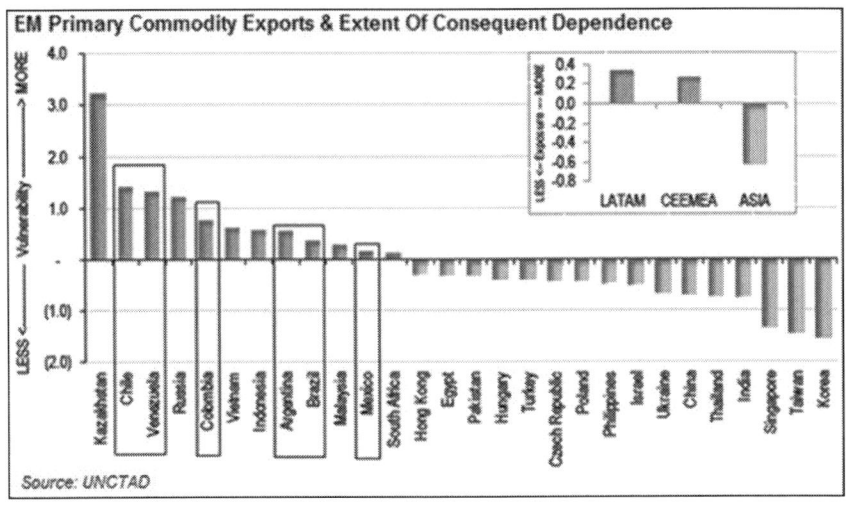

EM Primary Commodity Exports & Extent Of Consequent Dependence

Source: UNCTAD

In broad terms, of course, **all emerging markets can be regarded as the ultimate convergence trade,** in the same way that, for example, the valuations of eastern European countries in line for EU-accession gradually began to align with those of EU countries the nearer to the accession they drew (equities up, bond yields down, currencies strengthening). How far off an EM is from having converged into being a DM, of course, can mostly be seen from its credit rating (see earlier chart), aside from other tangential factors. Consequently, **they could be regarded as pure 'risk-on' trades, whatever the asset class involved. However, within this all-encompassing description, there has been a re-emergence of those EMs that can be regarded as further along the development path than all of the others and thus investable in a marginally risk-off environment.**

Prior to 2008, the former group was probably best symbolised by the **BRIC** group, comprised of Brazil, Russia, India and China, which led the way on EM valuations by dint principally of their projected growth paths. These were followed by the **Next-11** (Mexico, Indonesia, South Korea, Turkey, Bangladesh, Egypt, Nigeria, Pakistan, the Philippines, Vietnam and Iran), of which the first four of the grouping had consistently outperformed the remainder, earning the sobriquet of the **'MIST'** countries along the way.

In currency trading terms, investment in selected emerging markets can accrue the benefits both of carry compensation in the short-term (which may or may not show up directly on your trading P&L sheets, depending on the platform you are using, but will be reflected in the movement of the currency overall) and of growth prospects supporting real exchange rate appreciation over the longer term. The carry trade element of this is predicated, of course, upon the interplay of two key factors: wide (but stable) interest rate differentials (between the currency being sold to fund a higher-yielding currency) and low currency volatility on the first leg of the trade.

**Before the 2008 crisis, the rolling correlation between returns from a traditional carry basket and returns from the S&P500 fluctuated around zero in developed markets and positive for emerging markets currencies. In the most recent major 'risk-on' environment, though, it is interesting to note that the same rolling correlation for both developed and emerging markets moved into positive territory for some.** Consequently, in these cases, it might be said that either the emerging markets' currency carry trade risk converged to that of the developed markets' one or, more accurately, that this risk for developed markets' currencies moved up the risk curve towards a level more associated with an EM currency equivalent. Indeed, holding a carry basket today is almost the equivalent of holding a pre-crisis carry basket together with some S&P futures. Given this more level playing field on the risk side of the equation, then, attention tends to focus on the underlying fundamentals of EM countries now and on their projections going forward.

## *Emerging Markets Currencies*

From the purely currency perspective, emerging markets' assets will sometimes trend according to general RORO factors or to more local factors (political instability, specific economic concerns, the fortunes of their key export markets, for example) and it is necessary firstly to see where a specific currency falls in the RORO matrix, which can be accessed through a wide variety of websites and research available to everyone.

For example, a snapshot of currencies in Asia, Latin America and EMEA will tell you which currencies to trade based on RORO and which are dictated more by local factors, as seen below.

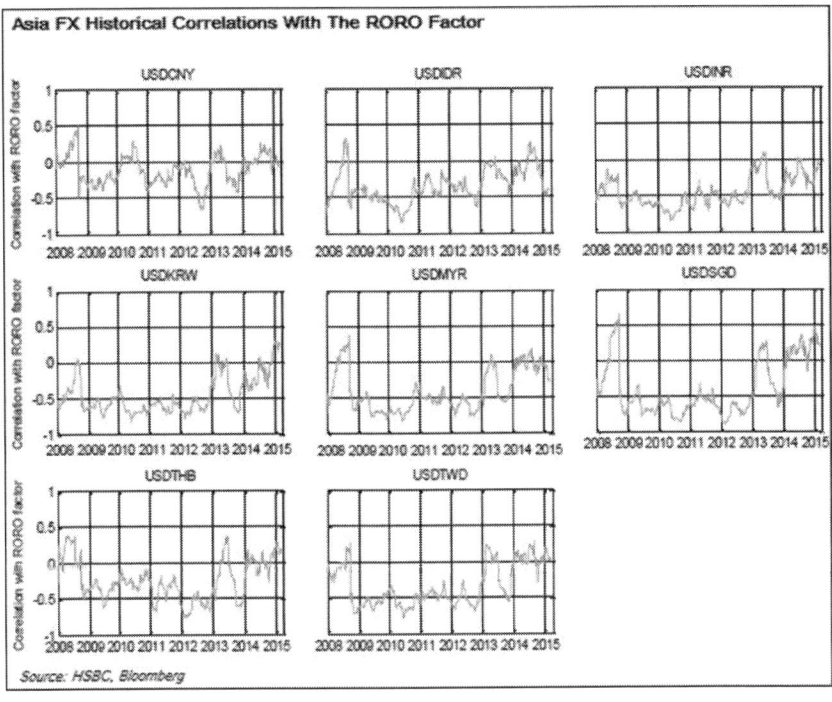

In Asia's case, it is interesting to note that much of the risk factor for those currencies demonstrating RORO correlations stems from the growth trajectory of the region's biggest economy, China. In this context, with concerns over the sustainability of the US economy still bubbling up from time to time to challenge the projected long-term uptrend of the USD, concerns over China's rate of growth are becoming more pronounced as well; as are those about Japan's and the eurozone's. Working out RORO, then, becomes more a case of judging which growth case scenario looks less bad than the rest of these major economic areas.

In this context, **China has accounted for around 50% of the world's total demand for all base metals and around 20% of its energy demand in the past ten years, but over that period the country's growth was heavily skewed towards manufacturing and infrastructure development, whereas in the most recent five year economic plan it has shifted its growth strategy towards being more consumer-led.**

This explains why there has been a **broad-based tightening of the correlation between all commodities prices in general (as shown on the Goldman Sachs Commodities Index, GSCI) and the Purchasing Managers Index (PMI)** – for both manufacturing and for services – coming out of China in the past few months.

Indeed, the PMIs seem to point not necessarily to a hard landing for China but certainly to a soft one that is not being driven by resource-intensive growth, such as building bridges, motorways, hospitals and so on; so, whereas we had a metals upwards pricing supercycle for a long while, cycles only work well in a manufacturing-based economy and not in a services-based one. Added to these factors, **there is one other that militates against a long-ranging rebound for commodities as a group: in an investment world dominated by a search for yield, commodities not only yield nothing whatsoever but actually cost investors money to hold.**

For Latin America, most of the currencies seen below are demonstrating a relatively low correlation to global RORO but rather are affected either by the oil price directly (Mexico) or indirectly (via lower prices for raw materials exports to consumer-led economies) and also by questions over China's growth trajectory and its type (the manufacturing-oriented/consumer-oriented mix, as it seeks to move away from the former type of growth towards the latter).

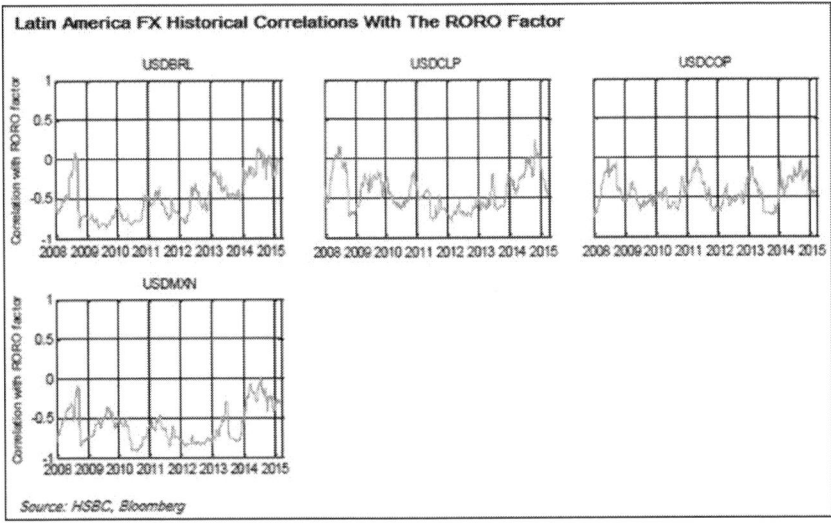

In broad terms, it could be said that the two countries' currencies that had the greatest exposure to China's uber-growth – the Chilean peso (CLP) and the Venezuelan bolivar (VEB) – are set to do worst in the coming few months as China's growth settles at a lower rate and changes in nature from a manufacturing-fuelled one to a consumer-led one.

However, more generally, **because the degree of investor involvement has been low, LatAm FX still appears to offer a risk-reward profile driven by individual stories that minimize global exposure and provide very clean positioning.** In this context, while LatAm FX was appreciating, the main concern of FX policies across the region was growth and thus the bias to intervene to weaken currencies, but the coin has now flipped and with LatAm FX now on a multi-year depreciation trend, sooner or later the focus of FX policy will shift to preventing pass-through pressures onto inflation.

All other factors being equal, the trade-weighted currencies that strengthen the most when the oil price rises are the Canadian dollar, Australian dollar and Brazilian real, joined by the South African rand (see below) and Indonesia rupiah, whilst the currencies that weaken the most are the US dollar, Chinese yuan, Indian rupee and the Japanese yen.

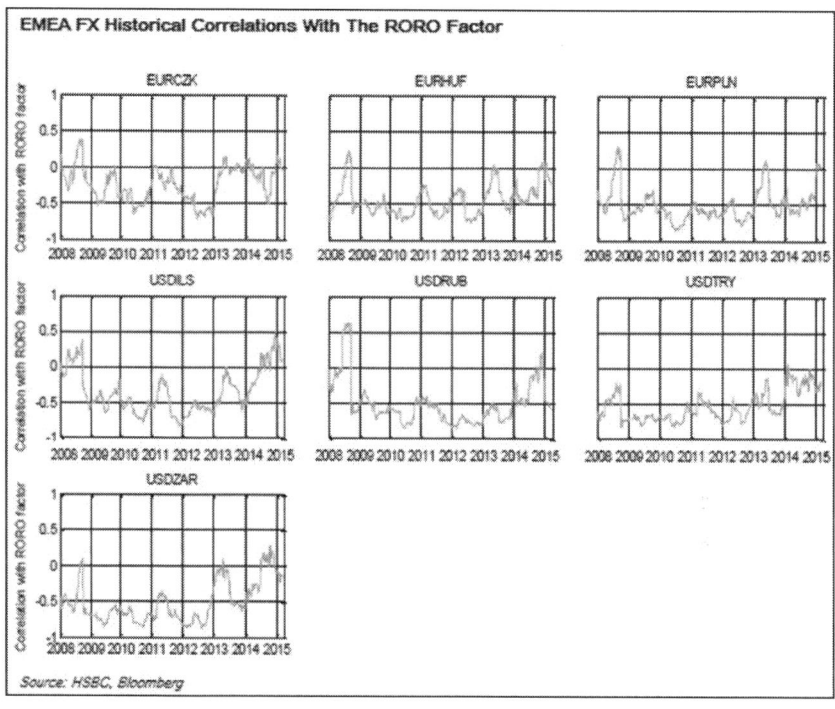

Overall, it is fair to say that any gaps in the developed markets' landscape are likely to be filled increasingly over time by the currencies of those emerging economies that meet **the basic criteria of an investment destination:**

1. **A sustainable fiscal policy.**
2. **A sound balance of payments profile.**
3. **A solid financial and political system.**

The **additional benefits of EM investment destinations is that more often than not they benefit both from momentum trading and carry trading strategies, given their relatively high interest rates in a broadly zero interest rate policy developed markets world.** In this context, it is highly likely in certain market conditions that incrementally value-added returns will be accrued from investment in the BRIC, MIST and N-11 countries over time simply as they converge towards developed markets status.

## *Emerging Markets Equities*

Having said all of this, the assumption that is still prevalent amongst global investors of all degrees of talent and experience – that an emerging market equity indices values will eventually converge into those of developed market ones – has not in fact been borne out historically, although from the pragmatic trading standpoint it is important to know the fact that the investment community largely believes the idea. **It is worth noting that it remains the case that just five of the 38 countries with stock markets in 1900 have moved from emerging to developed market status to date.** Of the rest, 17 were and are developed, 14 were and are classified as middle-income emerging and those with developed markets in 1900 still dominate the equity landscape, comprising 84% of the MSCI All World Index.

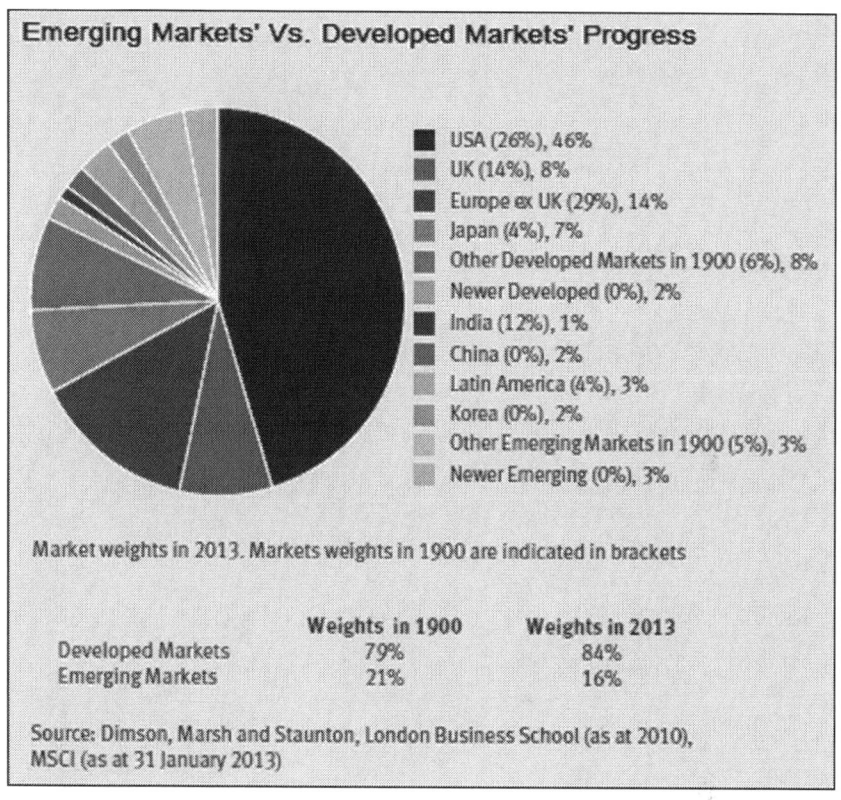

**Emerging Markets' Vs. Developed Markets' Progress**

- USA (26%), 46%
- UK (14%), 8%
- Europe ex UK (29%), 14%
- Japan (4%), 7%
- Other Developed Markets in 1900 (6%), 8%
- Newer Developed (0%), 2%
- India (12%), 1%
- China (0%), 2%
- Latin America (4%), 3%
- Korea (0%), 2%
- Other Emerging Markets in 1900 (5%), 3%
- Newer Emerging (0%), 3%

Market weights in 2013. Markets weights in 1900 are indicated in brackets

|  | Weights in 1900 | Weights in 2013 |
|---|---|---|
| Developed Markets | 79% | 84% |
| Emerging Markets | 21% | 16% |

Source: Dimson, Marsh and Staunton, London Business School (as at 2010), MSCI (as at 31 January 2013)

Moreover, academic research into the 'middle income trap', which assesses the likelihood of an economy progressing to DM status, suggests that the distribution of income also matters. **In this respect, the studies suggest that the more equal the distribution is (that is, the lower the GINI coefficient), the more likely a country is to move up from one level to another.** Other factors that influence development outcomes include the soundness of a country's institutions, progress on structural reforms and sustaining superior growth rates over the decades it would take for income levels to converge with those of developed markets. In this context, in aggregate, **the emerging markets did particularly well during the boom years of 2003-2007, rising from 20% to 34% of global GDP and from 4% to 10% of global equity markets but subsequently,**

**after an initial bounce in 2009, there has been little progress overall.**

## Emerging Markets' Progress

| GNI per Capita (USD) | | GINI coefficient | | Sovereign Credit Rating | |
|---|---|---|---|---|---|
| Singapore | *High Income* | Hungary | *Less than 40* | Hong Kong | *Investment Grade* |
| Ireland | | South Korea | | Ireland | |
| Hong Kong | | Greece | | Israel | |
| Israel | | Ireland | | Singapore | |
| Greece | | Poland | | South Korea | |
| South Korea | | India | | Poland | |
| Hungary | | Indonesia | | Brazil | |
| Poland | | Israel | | China | |
| Russia | *Upper Middle Income* | Turkey | *Greater than 40* | India | |
| Brazil | | Russia | | Malaysia | |
| Turkey | | Malaysia | | Mexico | |
| Mexico | | Singapore | | Russia | |
| Malaysia | | China | | South Africa | |
| South Africa | | Mexico | | Greece | *Junk* |
| China | | Brazil | | Hungary | |
| Indonesia | *Lower Middle Income* | Hong Kong | | Indonesia | |
| India | | South Africa | | Turkey | |

Source: The World Bank (as at 2011), Central Intelligence Agency World Factbook (as at 2012), Standard & Poors (as at 31 January 2013)

For a country to continue to enjoy enduring appeal to international investors – which creates a push effect on it achieving DM status over time (historically, markets tend to underperform the EM benchmark in the 12 months after an upgrade) – there needs to be a sea-change in the type of stocks available in which to invest. In this respect, entities that tend to list first and dominate domestic emerging market indices include former state-owned enterprises, resource companies and financials, which might not represent the more dynamic elements of the economy.

# Oil And Long-Term Global Economic Cycles

**Markets are subject to the manifestation of a wide variety of patterns; the key to trading success is identifying what they are and how to extract the optimal value from them.**

**In the simplest of terms, they can be looked at in terms of duration:** there are short-term patterns that mostly relate to technical analysis and there are longer-term ones that generally relate to broad economic factors (such as interest rates, inflation, GDP growth and so forth).

However, even beyond these, **there are broad-based long-term cycles** that relate to all of the above: **in technical analysis terms, for example, the Elliott Wave** (as described in the *Technical Analysis* section) is a good example; and in **economic terms the convergence of an economy** from 'frontier' market status to 'emerging' and then to 'developed' is another (as analysed earlier).

With regards to the oil price, all of these patterns and correlations find more resonance than in any other commodity market.

## Oil Price Cycles

In general terms, **it is apposite to note that previous cycles in the oil price were marked to a high degree by long time lags between when capital was spent and when production increased. However, the advent of widespread, well-funded shale technology has narrowed this time lag and concomitantly, given very high decline rates, producers' ability to quickly** throttle back production has also increased, which has provided the market with more levers for rebalancing in terms of credit, equity and cash flow.

The short-cycle nature of shale and its ability to ramp up production quickly requires that price pressure remains in place long enough to sideline the large amount of low cost capital available until that rebalancing occurs, as highlighted earlier, and the entire industry is re-pricing as costs decline and further efficiency gains are made. The level of uncertainty cannot be underestimated as these dynamics spill over into the price of commodities, currencies and consumption baskets around the world (as shown in the *Correlation* sections), with major long-term market and economic implications, which also find material directions from longstanding macroeconomic cycles.

## Current Cycle Vs 1986, 1981/82 and 2009/10

The **current pattern of oil price trading is perhaps most closely similar to that of 1986 in that it was also a predominantly supply-driven sharp decline in prices, rather than to the 1981-82 and 2009-2010 drop in prices, which were primarily demand-driven as the recessions led to a fall in global demand of more than 3 mbpd.** At the time, non-OPEC production was growing as well but the combined impact of both of these factors was offset by a sharp fall in OPEC volumes. As the world emerged from the recession global demand recovered gradually, adding around 1.5 mbpd in total over the period 1983-85, but this coincided with a period of strong non-OPEC growth, which in turn added 3 mbpd over the same period and put further pressure on OPEC's market share.

| The 1986 price collapse: Supply, demand and price dynamics (mbpd) | | | | | | | | | | |
|---|---|---|---|---|---|---|---|---|---|---|
| | 1980 | 1981 | 1982 | 1983 | 1984 | 1985 | 1986 | 1987 | 1988 | 1989 |
| Brent avg., USD/bbl | 38 | 37 | 33 | 30 | 29 | 28 | 15 | 18 | 15 | 18 |
| Global demand | 61.2 | 59.4 | 57.8 | 57.6 | 58.9 | 59.2 | 61.0 | 62.3 | 64.2 | 65.6 |
| Non-OPEC output | 36.9 | 37.7 | 38.6 | 39.7 | 41.2 | 41.6 | 41.9 | 42.4 | 42.4 | 41.8 |
| OPEC output (inc. NGLs) | 26.0 | 21.9 | 18.8 | 16.9 | 16.5 | 15.9 | 18.5 | 18.4 | 20.7 | 22.2 |
| OPEC share | 42.5% | 36.9% | 32.4% | 29.4% | 28.1% | 26.8% | 30.4% | 29.5% | 32.2% | 33.8% |
| change y/y | | | | | | | | | | |
| Global demand | | -1.8 | -1.6 | -0.2 | 1.3 | 0.4 | 1.7 | 1.3 | 2.0 | 1.3 |
| Non-OPEC output | | 0.7 | 0.9 | 1.1 | 1.5 | 0.4 | 0.3 | 0.5 | 0.0 | -0.6 |
| OPEC output | | -4.1 | -3.1 | -1.8 | -0.4 | -0.7 | 2.6 | -0.2 | 2.3 | 1.5 |
| change % | | | | | | | | | | |
| Global demand | | -3.0% | -2.7% | -0.4% | 2.2% | 0.7% | 2.9% | 2.1% | 3.1% | 2.1% |
| Non-OPEC output | | 2.0% | 2.4% | 2.9% | 3.8% | 1.0% | 0.8% | 1.1% | 0.1% | -1.4% |
| OPEC output | | -15.9% | -14.3% | -9.7% | -2.4% | -4.0% | 16.7% | -0.9% | 12.7% | 7.3% |
| Source: BP Statistical Review Of World Energy | | | | | | | | | | |

Within OPEC, combined production from Iraq and Iran had fallen by more than 6 mbpd through 1979-81, with the impact of the Iranian revolution and the start of the Iran/Iraq war. However, it then recovered by nearly 1.5 mbpd from 1981-85. The bulk of the sharp cutback in total OPEC output over this period was borne by Saudi Arabia, which cut output from roughly 10 mbpd in 1980-81 to average only some 3.6 mbpd in 1985. **However, in 2H 1985, in the face of steady growth in non-OPEC supply, Saudi Arabia abandoned its role as swing producer and pushed instead to regain market share, growing output to over 5mbd in 1986; very similar to the stance on its swing producer role that it has taken in recent months.** For OPEC as a whole, output rose by some 2.6 mbpd in 1986.

Overall, then, the result of this process was a collapse in Brent prices to a 1H86 average of sub-USD13/bbl vs a FY1985 average of close to USD30/bbl. However, this in turn spurred a prolonged period of demand strength, with global demand growing by an average of 2.4% over the period 1985-90. In addition, the crash in prices had a dramatic effect on non-OPEC investment levels, with the result that non-OPEC showed minimal overall growth in the second half of the 1980s.

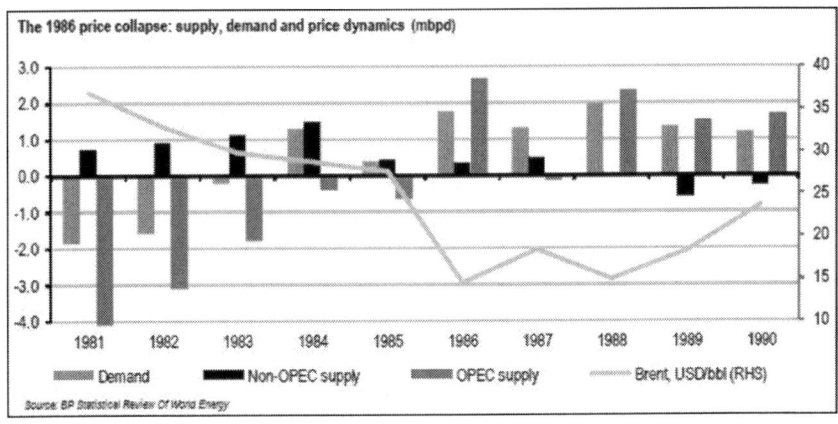

In this current oil market cycle, **there are a couple of reasons why prices are more inclined to revert to higher levels than occurred relative to 1985-88.** Firstly, although total non-OPEC output is currently around 20% greater than it was in the mid-1980s, it is also far more mature (the early/mid-1980s was the peak growth period for UK North Sea output and the previous peak for output in the US), so the non-OPEC production base now has much greater inherent decline rates due to this maturity and is thus more prone to a slowdown in investment.

Secondly, OPEC discipline is likely to be driven by the dramatic rise in crude prices required for economic stability in the various OPEC members (see earlier), with most market players thinking that, in the long run, prices of at least in the USD90s/bbl are needed to fill these requirements for countries such as Saudi Arabia and many of the other key OPEC producers.

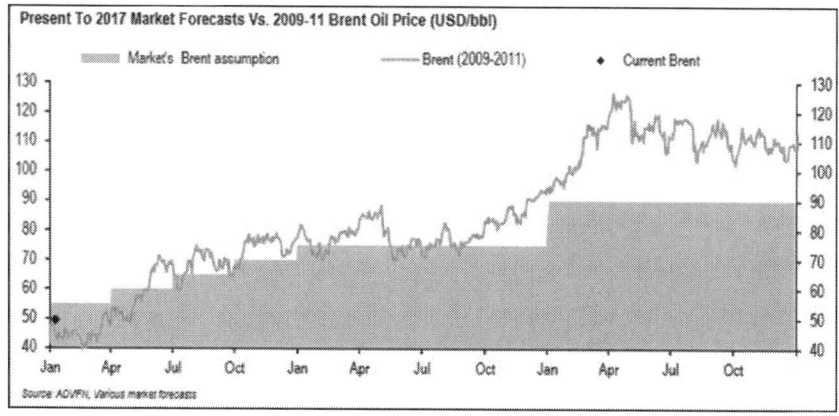

Of, course, **in the short- to medium-term, much depends on Saudi Arabia on the supply side and, in this respect, the Kingdom recently announced a budget that is based on USD60-70/bbl of Brent but even this is subject to substantial uncertainty as to what the country's cost basis is.** The riyal is pegged to the US dollar but Saudi imports European goods that have substantially declined in cost due to the falling euro. Saudi also imports agricultural products that have prices heavily tied to the Brazilian real and basic materials heavily tied to the Australian dollar. Iron ore is also facing efficiency gains, as is copper. So clearly, even a country like Saudi Arabia faces substantial uncertainties in balancing external and fiscal budgets due to commodity price pressures.

**What Of The Commodities Supercycle?**

Despite much talk to the contrary, the much-discussed end of the commodities supercycle is unlikely to have happened already; rather, it just appears to have shifted into a different phase, which has been referred to by a range of notable market organisations as 'the age of the energy capital stock' and which was evident as far back as the 1920s in the US. According to this, when the energy capital stock cycle is high it is old, and when it is low it is young; spotting where it is in the cycle allows the identification of periods of incremental investment, which in turn correlates to periods of high and rising commodity prices. These investment phases are then followed by an exploitation phase for a total cycle of around 30 years. The entire cycle can be summed up as: 10 years and billions of USD to develop a new supply source and the next 15-20 years of little investment and production running smoothly. In these terms, the supercycle can be regarded as the supply cycle for commodities while the business cycle (see below) is the demand cycle for commodities, which is why it is important to note for current trading purposes that the current cycle (and oil pricing) is supply-driven (like 1986).

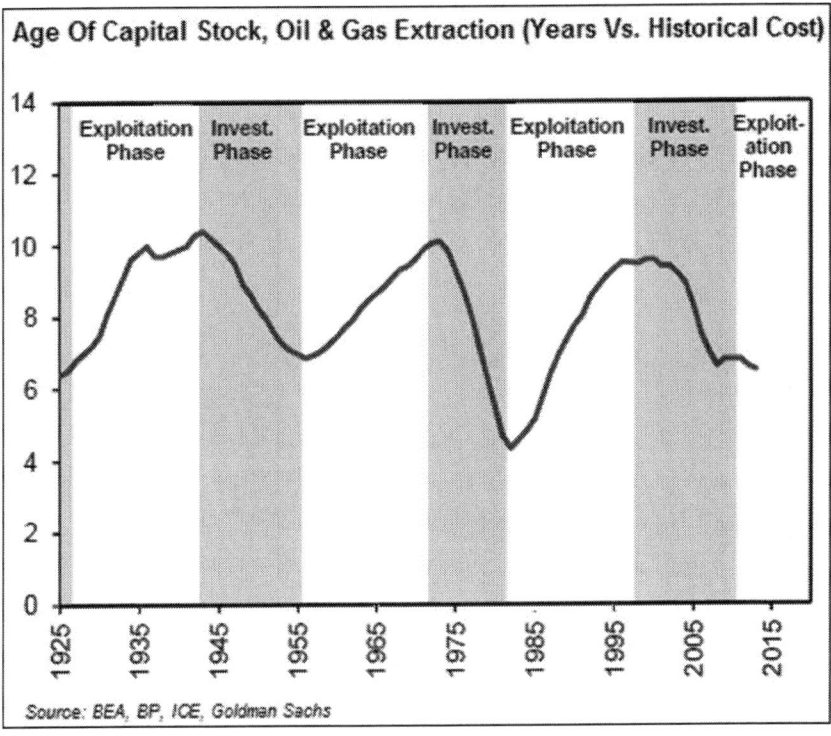

Looking at the charts above, **it is clear that during the investment phase, currency and commodity markets reinforced higher commodity prices and stronger emerging market growth, but today they are working in the other direction to support lower commodity and oil prices.** In this context, for example, a weaker

Chilean peso lowers the cost of producing copper via wages while lower energy prices also lower the overall costs as does the cheaper iron ore from Australia. The lower steel and copper prices in turn reduce the cost of producing energy and oil, and a lower oil price reinforces growth in the developed markets and helps to strengthen the US dollar.

**This is why identifying an equilibrium in one market is difficult without determining the equilibriums in the other commodity and currency markets.** Nonetheless commodity prices tend to decline during the exploitation phase, which is why commodity industries do not earn their cost of capital when looking at it over extremely long periods of time. They invest during high and rising commodity prices and produce during low and declining commodity prices (see chart below).

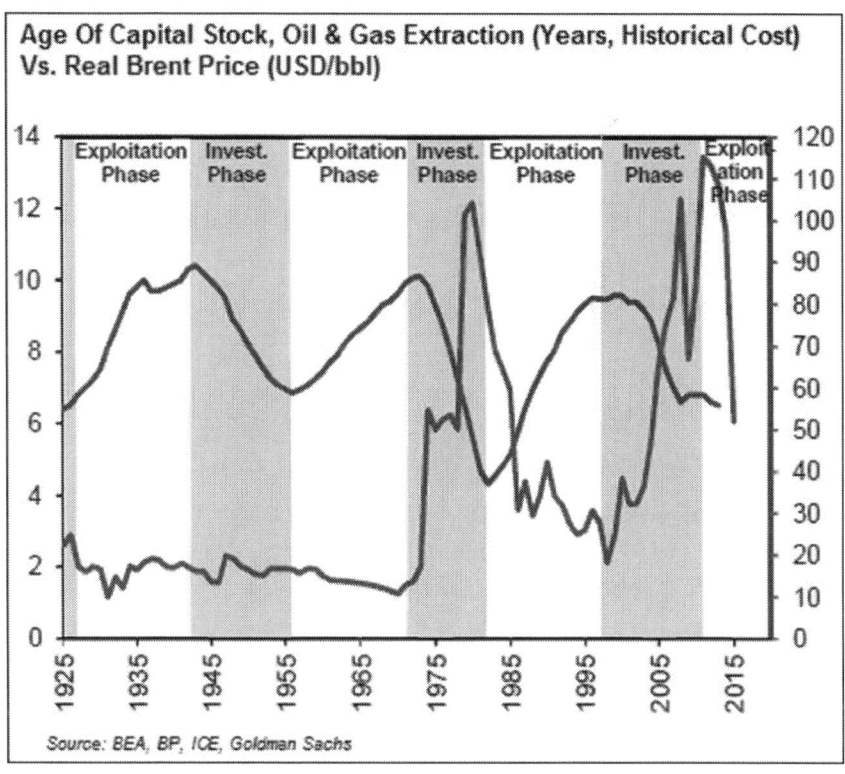

# Global Economic Cycles

## The Kondratieff Wave

In global terms (we will get to the specifics for regions and asset classes in a moment) to kick off with, the trader needs to be aware of the Kondratieff Wave ('K-Wave') – named after a Russian economist active in the 1920s named Nikolai Kondratieff – which seeks to show that **there are long-term cycles in the entire global capitalist economy of between 45 and 60 years (and even much longer) each that are self-correcting and evolving and are defined by the emergence of new industries in ongoing technological revolutions.** As an adjunct of this, each major cycle involves the destruction of much of the past cycle and the concomitant evolution of new innovation.

Kondratieff's theory has been refined/distorted – however you want to look at it – by various people since but the consensus of the major examples over the past few hundred years would be: the 1770s' Industrial Revolution, the 1820s start of the Steam and Railways age, the 1870s' Steel and Heavy Engineering move, the 1900s' era of Oil, Electricity, Automobiles and Mass Production and the 1970s' shift to the age of Information and Telecommunications.

It is interesting to note at this point that – arguably, although not much – the world's most successful stock investor ever, Warren Buffett, bases his investment strategy on such fundamental paradigmatic shifts; seeking to identify the onset of a new cycle (or 'wave'), buying shares in as many solid new cycle-related businesses as he can and just sitting on them.

It is also interesting to note, as we touched on Elliott Waves just a moment earlier, that we could regard the nature of these cycles in Elliott Waves' terms.

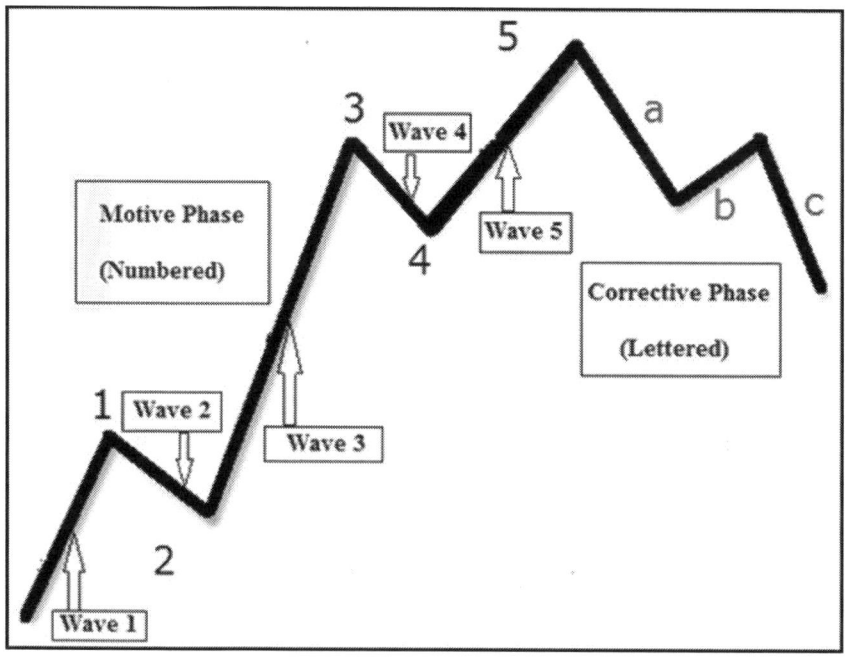

That is, that at the onset of a long-term economic cycle there is likely to be a lack of confidence and a fear of falling back into slump or depression, before inflation, interest rates and credit slowly start to rise as confidence in the new age increases (you might say, Elliott Wave 1).

As the economy expands (indicated in this instance by inflation) and interest rates increase as an adjunct to this, then so business and consumer confidence grows further and credit is extended more (Elliott Wave 3 correlation).

As we enter into the final up-phase of the move, confidence levels morph into over-exuberance and extraordinary loose 'bubble-like' credit conditions, with interest rates also declining (Elliott Wave 5 correlation).

Finally, rising concerns over loose credit, inflationary upward spiral and bad debt causes business and consumer reticence to embark on new projects (in business terms, expansion and in consumer terms, new purchases), default rates increase, credit is squeezed, the economic outlook turns negative, unemployment rises, disinflation turns into deflation and we have a negative world view.

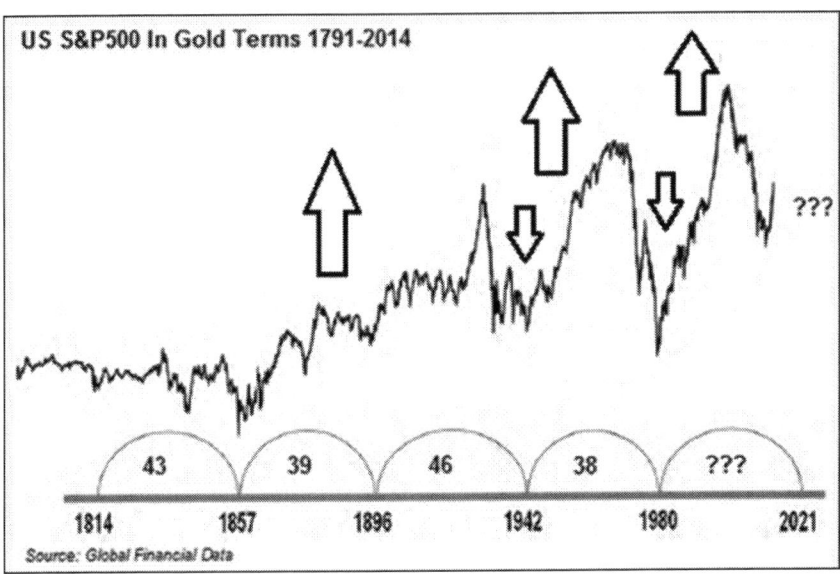

Consequently, it would be fair to say that based on this time set the **US stock market, and for that matter the UK one and those of the major northern European countries, are currently in an overall cyclical downturn and that, for the time being, the overall trend – economically and in terms of asset prices, interest rates and volatility – will be net down over the next few years.**

The Business Cycle

**Within this, though, there are other shorter-time patterns manifesting themselves in the classic business cycle,** which is the recurring level of business activity that changes in an economy over a period of time. The four stages of a cycle (although some maintain that there are five) are: full scale recession, early recovery, late recovery and early recession.

**Since the Second World War, most business cycles have lasted between three to five years from peak to peak,** with the average duration of an expansion being nearly four years and the average length of a recession being just under a year, although as we have seen in the most recent recession (and in the Great Depression era) recessions can last a lot longer.

According to the USA's National Bureau of Economic Research (NBER), the US has experienced 12 recessions (including the most recent one) and 11 expansions since the end of the Second World War.

## US Business Cycles Since 1857 (NBER)

| BUSINESS CYCLE REFERENCE DATES | | DURATION IN MONTHS | | |
|---|---|---|---|---|
| Peak | Trough | Contraction | Expansion | Cycle |
| Quarterly dates are in parentheses | | Peak to Trough | Previous trough to this peak | Trough from Previous Trough | Peak from Previous Peak |
| | December 1854 (IV) | -- | -- | -- | -- |
| June 1857(II) | December 1858 (IV) | 18 | 30 | 48 | -- |
| October 1860(III) | June 1861 (III) | 8 | 22 | 30 | 40 |
| April 1865(I) | December 1867 (I) | 32 | 46 | 78 | 54 |
| June 1869(II) | December 1870 (IV) | 18 | 18 | 36 | 50 |
| October 1873(III) | March 1879 (I) | 65 | 34 | 99 | 52 |
| March 1882(I) | May 1885 (II) | 38 | 36 | 74 | 101 |
| March 1887(II) | April 1888 (I) | 13 | 22 | 35 | 60 |
| July 1890(III) | May 1891 (II) | 10 | 27 | 37 | 40 |
| January 1893(I) | June 1894 (II) | 17 | 20 | 37 | 30 |
| December 1895(IV) | June 1897 (II) | 18 | 18 | 36 | 35 |
| June 1899(III) | December 1900 (IV) | 18 | 24 | 42 | 42 |
| September 1902(IV) | August 1904 (III) | 23 | 21 | 44 | 39 |
| May 1907(II) | June 1908 (II) | 13 | 33 | 46 | 56 |
| January 1910(I) | January 1912 (IV) | 24 | 19 | 43 | 32 |
| January 1913(I) | December 1914 (IV) | 23 | 12 | 35 | 36 |
| August 1918(III) | March 1919 (I) | 7 | 44 | 51 | 67 |
| January 1920(I) | July 1921 (III) | 18 | 10 | 28 | 17 |
| May 1923(II) | July 1924 (III) | 14 | 22 | 36 | 40 |
| October 1926(III) | November 1927 (IV) | 13 | 27 | 40 | 41 |
| August 1929(III) | March 1933 (I) | 43 | 21 | 64 | 34 |
| May 1937(II) | June 1938 (II) | 13 | 50 | 63 | 93 |
| February 1945(I) | October 1945 (IV) | 8 | 80 | 88 | 93 |
| November 1948(IV) | October 1949 (IV) | 11 | 37 | 48 | 45 |
| July 1953(II) | May 1954 (II) | 10 | 45 | 55 | 56 |
| August 1957(III) | April 1958 (II) | 8 | 39 | 47 | 49 |
| April 1960(II) | February 1961 (I) | 10 | 24 | 34 | 32 |
| December 1969(IV) | November 1970 (IV) | 11 | 106 | 117 | 116 |
| November 1973(IV) | March 1975 (I) | 16 | 36 | 52 | 47 |
| January 1980(I) | July 1980 (III) | 6 | 58 | 64 | 74 |
| July 1981(III) | November 1982 (IV) | 16 | 12 | 28 | 18 |
| July 1990(III) | March 1991(I) | 8 | 92 | 100 | 108 |
| March 2001(I) | November 2001 (IV) | 8 | 120 | 128 | 128 |
| December 2007 (IV) | June 2009 (II) | 18 | 73 | 91 | 81 |

| Average, all cycles: | Contraction | Expansion | Cycle | |
|---|---|---|---|---|
| 1854-2009 (33 cycles) | 17.5 | 38.7 | 56.2 | 56.4* |
| 1854-1919 (16 cycles) | 21.6 | 26.6 | 48.2 | 48.9** |
| 1919-1945 (6 cycles) | 18.2 | 35.0 | 53.2 | 53.0 |
| 1945-2009 (11 cycles) | 11.1 | 58.4 | 69.5 | 68.5 |

\* 32 cycles
\*\* 15 cycles
Source: NBER

Having said that, as mentioned earlier – particularly in the section looking at emerging markets – **different regions and countries within regions are not all at the same point of their overall business cycle, despite their being part of the long-running K Waves** that have to do with being in the global economy.

## Emerging Asia And Latin America

China aside (because although in strict Elliott Wave terms it looks to be on an upward wave, there are many more basic questions over the sustainability of its debt profile as discussed earlier), **emerging Asia has many markets that are in a long-term secular bull run, with the standout ones currently being Taiwan and Vietnam,** although there are compelling arguments for many others (Philippines, Malaysia and Indonesia, and eventually India and Thailand).

In Taiwan, for example, following the almost two decade-long triangle wave IV, it appears to be increasingly evident that the cycle degree wave V is in operation, which means that, as long as 7685 holds as support on the TAIEX index the structure will stay bullish. For Vietnam, in the meantime, the Ho Chi Minh Stock index is subdividing in a powerful cycle degree wave III, with major support around the 490 level.

In Latin America, the **Brazilian stock market** has been underperforming global stock market indices since 2010 but now the price action is producing evidence that a new bull market may be beginning. As long as the 2013 low of 44,107 remains in place the technical structure would point to the cessation of the long period of consolidation from the 2010 high and indicate that a third wave higher should be underway; well above the all-time (2008) high of 73,920.

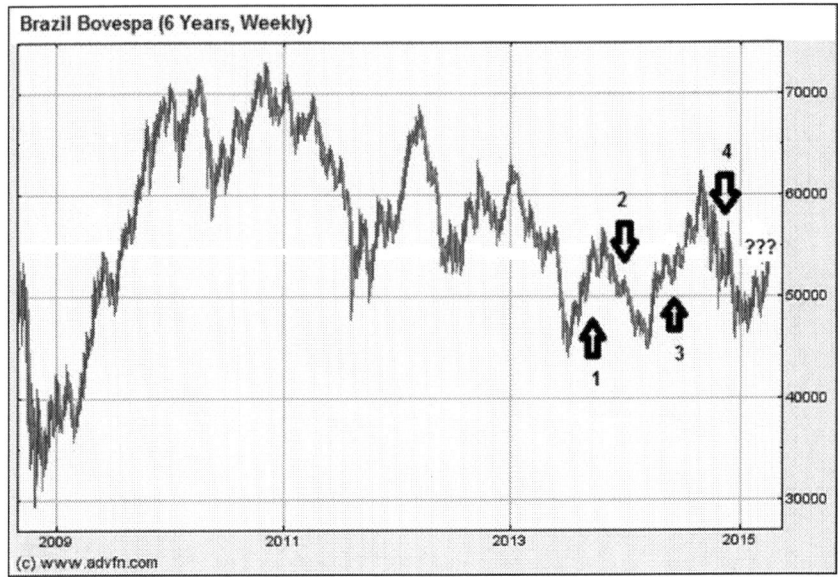

*[Chart Key:*
*Please see 'Elliott Waves' earlier]*

In the last book (*How To Make Big Money Trading In All Financial Conditions*), it was predicted, based on Elliott Wave Theory alone, that the **Mexican stock market** looked like the a-b-c Elliott Wave Correctional Move lower from the January 2013 high had been completed and that a new Motive Phase upwards might be beginning upwards, as shown by the chart below.

116

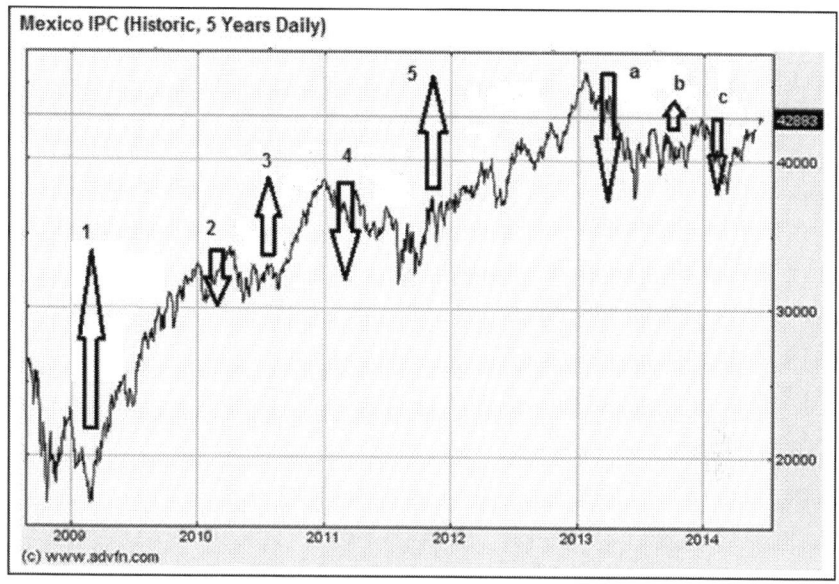

*[Chart Key:*
*Please see 'Elliott Waves' earlier]*

In fact, **this is precisely what happened,** as seen in the latest chart below.

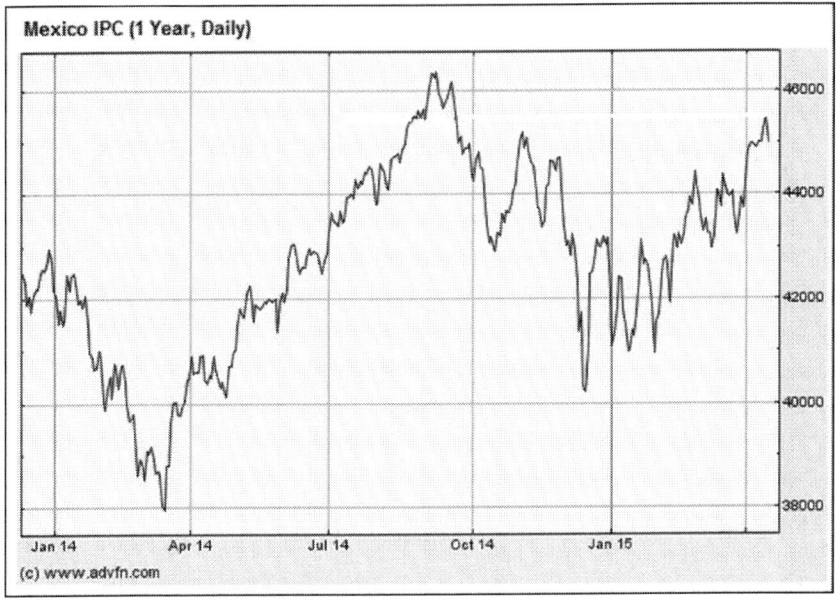

Mexico IPC (1 Year, Daily)

(c) www.advfn.com

[Chart Key:
Please see 'Elliott Waves' earlier]

## The Minsky Cycle

Markets move in patterns, as mentioned, and the 'Minsky Cycle' is another important element in the understanding of where one is in the overall global investment mix (which means, in practical terms, narrowing down the best trading options further) and is itself part of the broader Business Cycle, which is, in turn, part of the Kondratieff Wave (or cycle).

The Minsky Cycle – coined around the time of the 1998 Russian financial crisis by a guy from PIMCO (Pacific Investment Management Company) – is a key part of the general psychology of trading (see below) and **seeks to chart the nature of the normal life cycle of an economy with particular reference to speculative investment bubbles.**

The idea here is that in times of prosperity, when the cashflow of banks and corporations moves to excess levels (over and above that which is needed simply to pay off debt), a 'speculative euphoria' develops, which soon exceeds that which borrowers can pay off, which, in turn leads to tighter credit conditions etc. It is the slow pace at which the financial system moves to at first realise this and then seek to accommodate it that produces a financial crisis; known as the 'Minsky Moment'.

It is interesting to note here that knowing where one is in the cycle is crucial to making long-term, informed and extremely profitable positions, as is illustrated below in the shift along the Minsky Curve of what is propitious and what is not.

**Typical Minsky Cycle Characteristics**

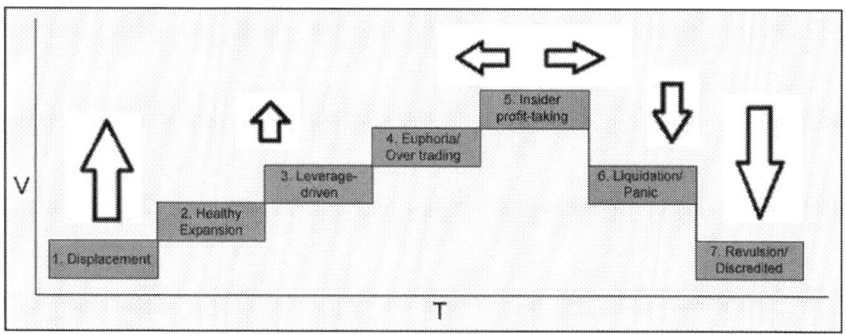

*[Chart Key:*
*V = Values, various assets*
*T = Time]*

So, looking at the above chart, for example, **in the immediate 'displacement' aftermath of the Great Financial Crisis, in the middle or so of 2011, one might have nascent identified pockets of value in Asian FX as various of the countries continued to show exceptional performance.** As the cycle progressed, the major beneficiaries of leverage became certain high-yielding currencies (such as the AUD) and certain commodities (notably, gold).

As credit became easier, so investors became less discerning about the underlying fundamentals of the assets into which they invested, and in the 'euphoria/over-trading' phase, for example poured money into various of the already over-performing equities markets (China springs to mind).

As ever in the markets, key insiders began to twig that a new indiscriminate phase of investment had manifested itself (the "when my gardener is talking to me about stocks then I know it's time to get out" concept), so liquidated out of things like Japanese government bonds and toppish currency positions.

And, once this has occurred, of course, there is a much broader liquidation of assets (at this point it included things like selling USD and gold), which, given the need to make good on losses in margin calls actually involves selling a much broader base of assets than would otherwise be merited.

Finally, the markets reach a point where investors are ultra-cautious in spending their money and regard any asset that is not rated as absolutely solid (CHF is usually a beneficiary of this collective state of mind, of course) as being, in fact, abhorrent, with the main loser at the end of this particular cycle being the debt and other assets of eurozone periphery countries.

**Looking at where we were in the middle of 2014, we can see that the displacement macro-shock had been negative rates announced by the ECB, the long and low easing policy of the US Fed appearing to be drawing to an end and a broad-based acceptance of an enduring economic slowdown in China gathering pace.**

Within this, different asset classes are at different points along that cycle: for example, the USD may be entering a new long-term uptrend, as mentioned earlier; the JPY appears to be nearing the 'discredited' phase (as dealers cannot see what more can be done to weaken the currency, given what has already been implemented to do so); whilst there has been a generalised liquidation of being long volatility (volatility can be bought or sold, like any other aspect of the market, either directly – say through the VIX and similar indices – or indirectly through proxies).

Given such an identification of which part of the cycle forms the backdrop to your current investment environment, **there are some general inferences that you can take regarding which sectors within – specifically – stock markets may prove the most beneficial at a particular point in time,** as delineated below:

- **Full Scale Recession** (characterised by contracting GDP quarter-on-quarter, falling interest rates, increasing unemployment, declining consumer expectations, among others). Sectors that do well in this environment tend to be: **Cyclicals** (a company's revenues are generally higher in periods of economic prosperity and expansion and lower in periods of economic downturn and contraction but they can cope easily by reducing wages and workforce during bad times and include companies that produce durable goods, such as raw materials and heavy equipment), **Transports, Technology and Industrials**.

- **Early Recovery** (consumer expectations are rising, unemployment is falling, industrial production is growing and interest rates have bottomed out): **Industrials, Basic materials industry and Energy firms**.

- **Late Recovery** (interest rates can be rising rapidly, consumer expectations are beginning to decline and industrial production is flat): **Energy, Staples and Services**.

- **Early Recession** (Consumer expectations are at their worst, industrial production is falling and interest rates are at their highest): **Services, Utilities, Cyclicals and Transports**.

# Brief Note On The Psychology Of Trading

## The Competition

As in life in general, in trading as well it is important to know who you are up against, because trading is a zero sum game as far as each individual is concerned: one either wins or one loses over time and, ultimately, it will always be at someone else's expense.

The market consists broadly of two types of investors: institutional ones and retail ones. The general parameters of this investment universe are simple enough: in 2009, it was measured that retail traders (RT) on average are responsible for about USD110 billion in currency flows across options, swaps, futures and spot forex in total per day; the figure for institutional investors (II), though, was around USD5.3 trillion, according to the last triennial FX Survey from the Bank for International Settlements in Basel (BIS).

More specifically, then, the retail investor would be well advised to learn how to read the psychology behind these institutional investment flows and ride along with them. However, within this idea, the retail investor also needs to recognise that not all institutional investors (II) are the same. Again, in broad terms, **one can regard IIs as being either 'Real Money Funds', which encompass those funds looking to generate steady, sustainable returns over time for their investors (such as pension funds, insurance companies and so on), and hedge funds, which, despite the conservative nature implied in the nomenclature, are usually at the end of sharper, shorter, more violent moves in the market.**

Trading in the euro over the past few years is very illustrative of the different tactics generally employed by both Real Money Funds and Hedge Funds.

## *Real Money Funds*

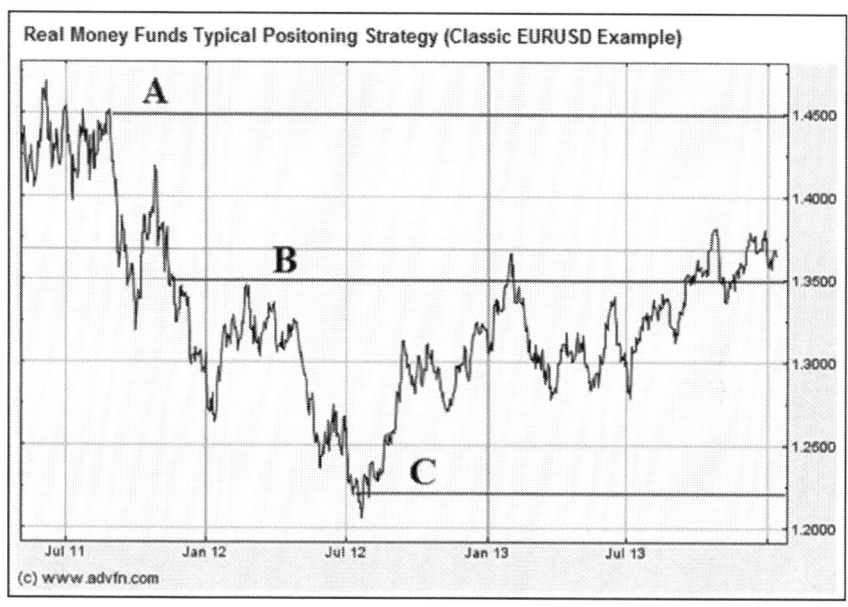

[Chart Key:
A = RMFs *sell EURUSD at 1.4500*
B = RMFs *take part-profit around 1.3500, so 7% return banked*
C = RMFs *buy back remainder @ 1.2200, so 16% profit all in*]

Each real money fund would have formed their own particular rationale underpinning why they should short the EUR but a common one at the time, and entirely reasonable, stemmed from the general thesis that the inhabitants of Europe do not broadly think of themselves in notional ideological terms as being 'European', or even Northern European or Southern European, but rather in practical nationalistic terms as being German, French, Italian and so on. In this profoundly basic context, the argument ran, a paradox lay at the heart of the European Union: it is designed to create a pan-European identity amongst a diverse range of peoples who fundamentally do not, and have never, seen themselves as anything other than citizens of nation states, each with their own individual language, culture, history and traditions.

Further still, this fundamental nationalism across EU states meant that there has always been an endemic reluctance on the part of the more industrialised and wealthier countries of Northern Europe to assist the softer economies of Southern Europe, particularly when they were regarded as profligate. So the argument would run, and the fundamental rationale for selling EURUSD was born.

## Hedge Funds

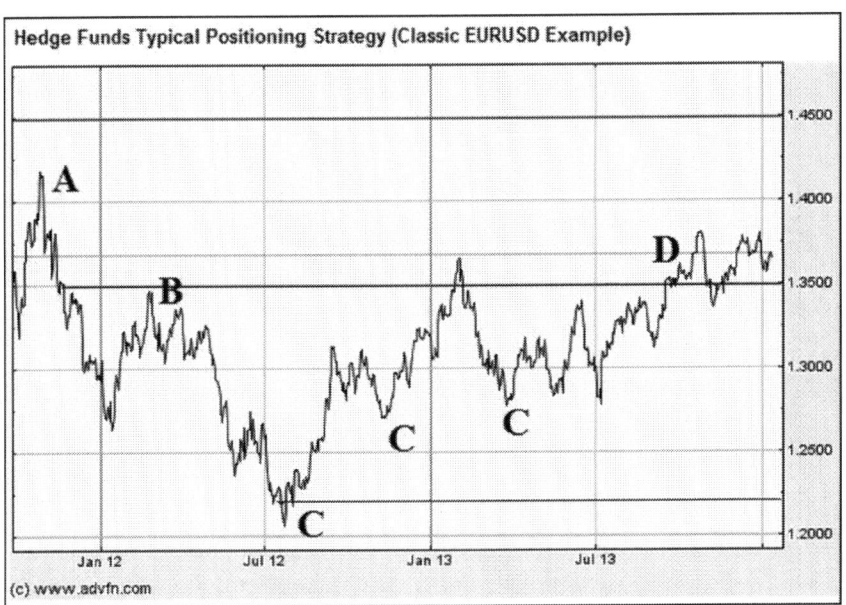

[Chart Key:
A = HFs sell at key technical resistance level
B = HFs sell again at next major technical level
C = HFs buy back shorts aggressively, morphing into going net long
D = HFs sell out all longs]

The above chart shows a number of key facets of hedge fund trading of which the RT needs to be aware. To begin with, it is wise to note that **the underlying rationale behind the trade may well have been the same as for the RM but hedge funds will add dynamic and aggressive intraday trading tactics to the mix.** In the above example, for instance, **most of the major moves happen overnight or in other periods in which the market is relatively illiquid.** This is a classic hedge fund strategy. It means that less money can have a disproportionately great effect on the price than in normal liquid conditions.

Another tactic frequently employed by hedge funds is to **trend the market in one direction, encouraging others (especially RT) to follow that trend, and then rapidly squaring off that position and simultaneously taking the opposite one.**

In this strategy, RTs can often find their positions going quickly against them, and then being stopped out (i.e. having to buy back EURUSD). Add all of these RT stops going through the market, in illiquid conditions, and you set the stage for a rapid move back up, which is what the hedge funds wanted.

A final point of which to be aware is that **hedge funds often choose to launch such ambushes at key technical levels, where they know RT investors will be watching closely for directional signs,** hence, in the above example, selling at major resistance levels, Fibonacci retracements and so forth. However, it is important to note that hedge funds often choose to reverse these positions at levels which apparently have no technical significance whatsoever, thus taking everyone by surprise and hijacking market momentum.

Once hedge funds get it into their collective minds to go after something that they perceive to be weak, then there is every chance that the move will be strong, so it is often a good idea to ride along with it for a while, especially if it aligns with genuine rationale for the trade.

## Greed And Fear

These are the two key emotions of which traders fall foul most often and, despite what Gordon Gekko (whose character, by the way, was reputedly based on an amalgam of one-time junk bond king Michael Milken and corporate raider Ivan Boesky – both of whom went to prison for a while) said, greed is not good and nor is fear.

**Greed manifests itself most palpably during bull trends, and the less experience/discipline a trader has, the more he is in danger of succumbing to its ill-effects on trading strategy.** In a bull trend, the key problem for the RT comes when he gets greedy for further profits (provided he is long) and decides to hold his position for that bit longer, just to capitalise on his good fortune. The logical outcome of this is that he will hold on to his position until such a point that the trade starts to reverse and go down. Unfortunately, particularly in FX, this turnaround can happen extremely quickly and all the more so if there is a significant presence of hedge fund money in the market (see above Hedge Fund chart).

At this point, the prevailing emotion is still greed, as the trader begins to fret that he has not taken all the profit he could and waits for his position to go back up again to the point at which he could have sold out and taken profit about five minutes earlier. Sod's Law here is that, of course, **it will continue to go down, at which point the RT's prevailing emotion starts to change to fear. Fear that he cannot get out of his position except at lower levels and greater fear as all his profit is wiped out and his position starts to go into the red.**

This is where the contents of the next section come in, which, together with Effective Order Placement and solid Technical Analysis, should form the cornerstone to the overall strategy of not getting caught out in the vicissitudes of greed and fear that will ultimately destroy a trading account.

The key point here sounds simple enough but it is extremely commonly ignored by inexperienced/ill-disciplined traders: **do not** run losses past a comfortable stop-loss point (with the order having gone in at the same time as the entry trade), only run profits.

## Trading Is A Lonely Occupation

By definition, retail trading is a lonely occupation, even if a trader is surrounded by a host of other traders, either in a bank or fund or in a purpose-built retail trading office, so if a would-be trader is a sociable sort he is better advised to choose a different occupation entirely.

**Loneliness during trading can have three major negative effects on a trader's profitability, if it is not recognised and managed effectively: first, it can make a trader question the validity underpinning a trade; second, it can lead to 'knee-jerk' trading, in which the RT nervously exits a perfectly sound position, changes direction, then trades out of that and so on; and third, sitting alone waiting for things to happen can cause a trader to trade out of boredom, and such trades invariably over time will wipe a trader out.**

In the event of the first and second scenarios, a trader should go back through the fundamental rationale for the trade, re-examine the technical levels (S&P, Fibonacci retracements, Moving Averages, RSI and so on), gauge prevailing market sentiment and if all of these are still sound then hold the position. In the third scenario, if the trade still appears sound, then do something else to pass the time (professional dealing rooms are full of traders doing 'something else' in order to avoid 'boredom trading').

**In any event, at exactly the same time as putting on an entry trade, a trader should at least put on the stop-loss trade as well so the downside is covered and putting on the take-profit order with the other two also means that the trader limits the danger of engaging in boredom trading, as he can leave his screens and do something else entirely.**

## Gap Trading

In a truly efficient market (one in which every participant knows the true price and what everyone else's position is, which is open all the time and so on), the ebb and flow of pricing would be seamless, up or down.

However, this is not always true, and **in some conditions markets tend to 'gap' – that is, they jump from one price to a much higher/lower level without trending up/down beforehand.** This is seen particularly in the less liquid markets and, consequently, is **often seen in the commodities markets in general and in the oil market as well, which are less liquid than both FX or many equities markets.**

Dynamic Of Gap Times (applies to a lesser degree to FX, which is 24/7 but slighter volumes will usually be noticed in these gap periods): Japanese and Asia and Australasia session 00:30-07:30 GMT/Gap Time 07:30-08:00 GMT, London and European Session 08:00-13:00 GMT/Gap Time 13:00-3:30 GMT, US Session 13:30-20:30 GMT/Gap Time 20:30-00:30 GMT.

It is apposite to note that the most liquid market is when the London and New York markets are open at the same time and the least liquid is when only Asia and Australasia are in the game.

This gap phenomenon usually appears in markets that are not 24/7 (as the FX market is). For example, if one is trading the FTSE100 then it is clear that there is a timing gap between when the FTSE closes on Friday and when it reopens on Monday morning at 8am GMT, as illustrated in the chart below.

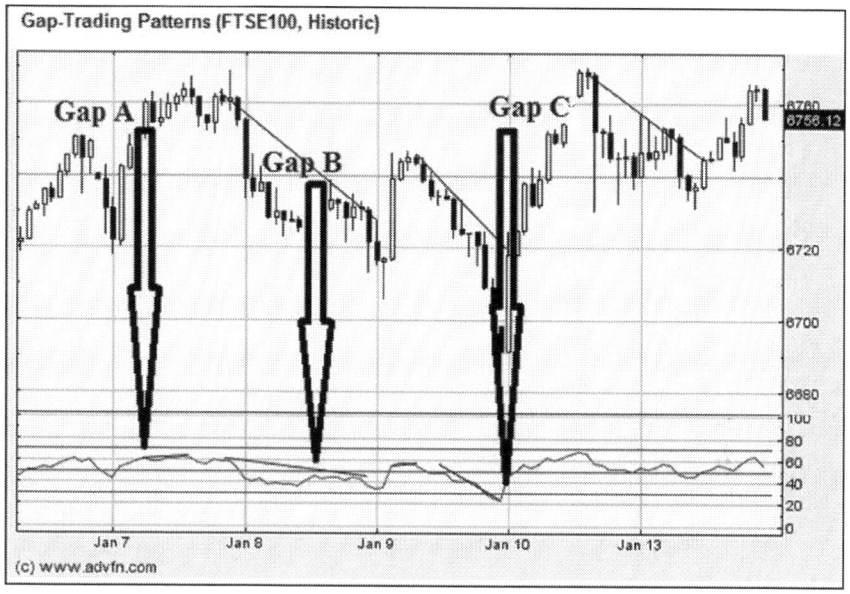

Gap-Trading Patterns (FTSE100, Historic)

[*Chart Key:*
*Gap A = RSI shows no real buying momentum — the smart money is looking to sell on rallies, whilst the hysterical money is chasing the tail of the last move up*
*Gap B = Same pattern as in the previous example — hysterical money is still convinced it is going up but smart money is not — hence the small candlesticks*
*Gap C = With a new week, the smart money has made its profits on shorts and is now going long — with more commitment shown by longer candlesticks]*

Above it can be seen from the RSI trends that there is only one real move up based on 'smart money': that punctuated by Gap 3. In the latter event, the 'hysterical money' is chasing the tail of the move or incorrectly anticipating the level at which the smart money may take profits on shorts.

In smart money moves, the candlesticks themselves tend to be bigger than in hysterical money moves, which are shorter and often punctuated by small reversals (lack of confidence in one's fundamental positioning).

With Gap Trading, though, even as an RT good money can be made by correctly identifying the overall trend, both from the price action on the foremost graph and from the underlying momentum underpinning the trade trend (from RSI, Price Oscillator, MACD and so on).

**In determining which way the smart money – or more particularly, the weight of smart money – is going, a good tool is to regard charts as combinations of 'impulse' moves and 'corrective' moves.** In this context, in short, an impulsive move is one that covers more pips in less time than a corrective one. Additionally, impulsive moves are characterised by longer candlesticks than corrective ones. And finally, impulse moves comprise several of the same coloured candlesticks in a row.

Conversely, a corrective move is characterised by a more even distribution of bull and bear candlesticks and by the emergence of more wicks/tails on the candle's extreme points. Additionally, a corrective move will be made up of a more balanced mixture of winning candlesticks against losing ones (i.e. the number of pips made against the number of pips lost).

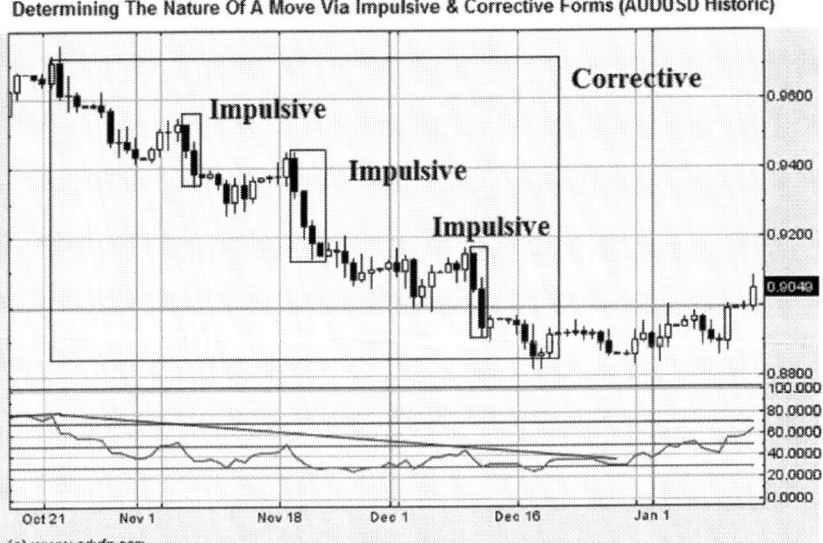

Determining The Nature Of A Move Via Impulsive & Corrective Forms (AUDUSD Historic)

As in the chart above, it is clear that the move down on AUDUSD had heavy money behind it, eventually both a mixture of broad-based corrective moves and of sudden impulsive moves on the back of those, and it was not going to turn on short-term RTs trading against it. In this respect it is rather similar to trying to stop a charging bull elephant with a pea-shooter.

In summary, the overall downmove covered by the corrective pattern box above was 848 pips but, as can be seen, three of these one-way (impulse pattern) moves accounted for 646 pips of that. The impulsive moves were marked, as mentioned, by one-way trading (back to back black candles in this diagram, denoting selling) that are much longer than the bid candles showing fast, determined price action.

A generally sound policy to find a good entry position for the day ahead is to **watch the market for around half an hour before the start of the session** (in the case of FX in London, you should be watching it from around 6am GMT at the latest).

If the **price drops below the most recent significant low but does not hold there for more than a few minutes (tops) then a rule of thumb is that players are trying to find better levels to go long/add to long positions** by temporarily selling the currency pair down in slim market volume conditions.

Therefore, **taking into account all the preparation of support and resistance levels, general economic and political overview, RSI analysis, MACD** etc, if a long still makes sense then go long when the price starts to dip down to the level at which you think the other players were trying to get long. And, of course, the reverse is true.

In this context, the breaking of recent lows and highs at the beginning/end of a session is often a signal of opposite orders being filled at a better price. This will tell you where the smart money is positioning itself (together with the other factors discussed above).

In the above example, of course, make use of effective order management, as previously discussed.

## Contrarian Trading

The key to this type of trading is to **look at the markets in terms of the sentiment of those participating in it, to gauge when is the right time to buy and when the right time to sell and to use correct risk management techniques.** Looking at the first point, sentiment underpinning a trend can be gleaned, among other things, from the 'Commitment of Traders Report' (COT), which is available for free download from the Commodities Futures Trading Commission (CFTC) website; for the energy sector, it is at the following, to be precise: http://www.cmegroup.com/trading/energy/cftc-tff/main.html.
Although this is data that applies specifically to the futures market, there are other COTs on the same site dealing with all other major asset classes (and they are updated every Friday).

Basically, the usefulness of the COT is that it shows the net long/short positions for every available futures contract for commercial traders (hedgers) and non-commercial traders (speculators, including currency traders, equities traders and commodities traders). As some of these futures contracts are simply hedges against real tangible positions (energy companies buying oil futures, for example) **these contracts give excellent indications of powerful trends at one extreme end of the market.**

## Producer Positioning In Oil Futures (CME COT, End April 2015)

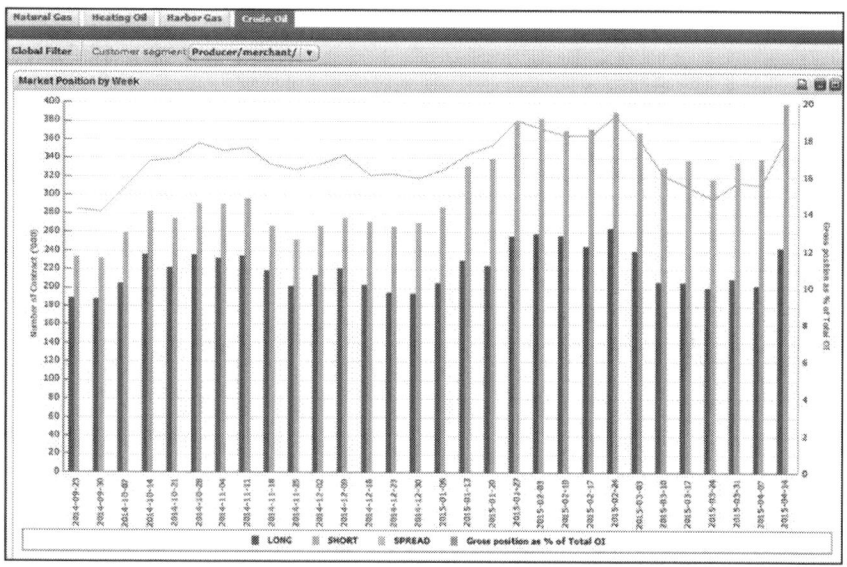

For the energy sector Hedge Funds' positions – and Real Money ones – these show up as 'Managed Money', whilst in other asset classes they are separated out further, with Hedge Funds shown as 'Leveraged Money' and Real Money Funds shown as 'Asset Manager'.

Above it can be seen that there is a large combined short for futures contracts for oil by the producers of it, which shows that they are selling it forward for legitimate supply and hedging purposes for higher prices than currently. This is in stark contrast to the positioning of fund management companies as shown below, which – with huge longs – shows that they believe that prices will eventually rise even further over time, past the shorter contract dates.

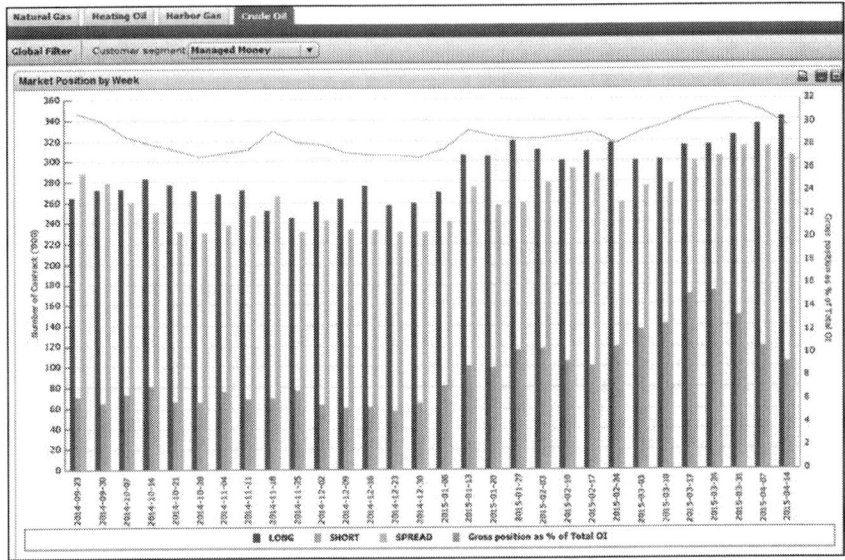

As a rule of thumb, speculators tend to buy the market when it is still rising whereas hedgers tend to sell into any rises (and vice-versa for a falling market, of course). In a rising market, therefore, when hedgers bets are increasing substantially and/or those of speculators, are diminishing in tandem, then the top of the market cannot be that far away.

This is why it is important to use other technical indicators to assess exactly at what level one is going to exit a long position or enter a new short position.

## The VIX

The Volatility Index (VIX) measures the implied (not historic) volatility of the options bought and sold on the S&P500 US stock index. The VIX can be found on the Chicago Board Options Exchange (CBOE) website, under the symbol 'VIX'.

In broad terms, of course, volatility is a measure of deviation of market prices from the average mean price over a specified period of time, achieved by looking at Moving Averages. Moving averages, to recap, are simply each day's price added together and then divided by a certain number of days, and **are particularly useful in determining short-term indications as to whether a market is set to continue in its current trend, reverse that trend or trade in a range.** As an additional confirmation (to established support and resistance levels, for instance), they offer a good idea of whether an asset is likely to break to the topside or the downside.

Given that options are usually associated with hedging positions against adverse price movements (normally, therefore, they can be seen as protection against a reversal in the present trend) then one can assume that generally the greater the VIX, the greater the fear amongst followers of trend only that a reversal is on the cards. At this point, a position can be liquidated (or opposite position put into place) or the RT can examine other trading options.

**CBOE Volatility Index (VIX) Is A Good Indicator Of Some Trend Reversals**

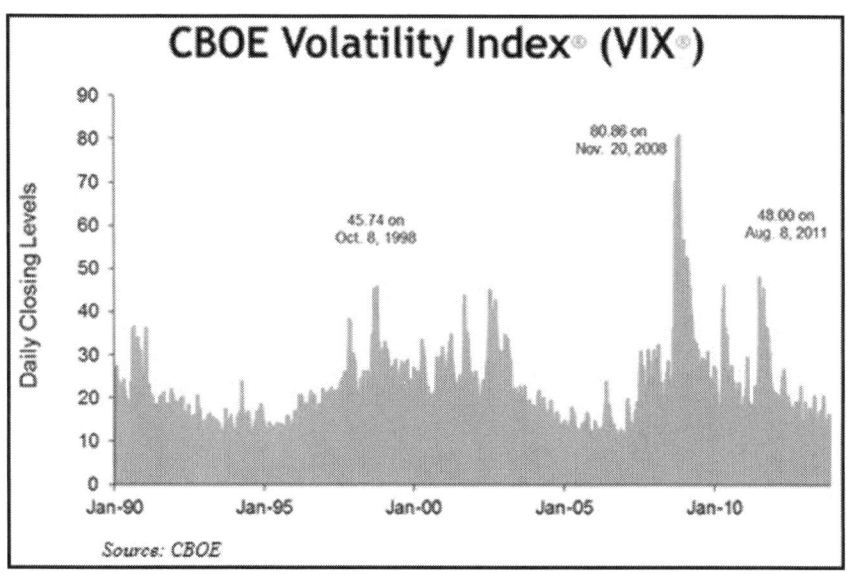

# Risk/Reward Management And Hedging

## The Nature Of Risk

Ultimately, money goes to where it is best rewarded (yielded from interest rates) for the concomitant risks involved (indicated by credit ratings) and this is, broadly speaking, the definition of the 'risk curve'. **Traders, in order to be successful over time, need to be constantly aware of this risk curve and also to manage the risk/reward ratio of their own investment portfolio in a logical, sensible and emotionless fashion. Otherwise, they will go broke. It is as simple as that.**

In the case of **in-the-money (ITM) positions,** bad traders (i.e. those not managing their risk properly) exit at the wrong time, either getting out once the peak profit-taking opportunity has passed (through misplaced greed) or getting nervous and taking profit way before they should. In the case of **out-of-the-money positions (OTM),** they hang on to bad positions hoping that they will turn around. The key guiding principle here, as mentioned before, is **do not run losses past a comfortable stop-loss point (with the order having gone in at the same time as the entry trade), only run profits.**

**By far the best way for a retail trader to avoid being one of the 90% of this breed that loses all his money within 90 days of starting to trade is by utilising – and religiously sticking to – orders (both stop-loss and take-profit) when trading,** and we look at this in depth below.

# The Risk Curve

The more risk involved in an asset, the more reward (interest rate) is required. Hence, the worse an economy is perceived to be doing the more reward investors will want as compensation to holding an asset if that country. By extension, if that interest rate does not increase then that asset will be unpopular and thus weak.

**Having said that, there is a** major difference between probability and a risk/reward profile in trading terms.

The law of probability (more accurately, the 'Law of Large Numbers') is:

"If the probability of a given outcome to an event is P and the event is repeated N times then the larger N becomes, so the likelihood increases that the closer, in proportion, will be the occurrence of the given outcome to N*P."

In practical terms, this means really that if a two-sided coin is tossed a sufficient number of times then the distribution of the results between heads coming up and tails coming up will be exactly the same.

There is an evident problem here for the trader: there is a 50/50 chance on the first toss that heads will come up and, therefore, according to the logical extension of what many 'trader training companies' say, it would be perfectly reasonably to put half your money on heads but – having put money on this outcome – it instead comes up tails. Nonetheless, according to the aforementioned rationale, the trader then puts everything on heads coming up, as given that tails came up first time and the probability of heads coming up was 50% (1 in 2) heads is bound to come up next time but it does not and, continuing to pursue this rationale, the trader will go broke.

**The fact is that probability only goes a part of the way to explaining sequences of numbers** (which is what any trading actually is).

There is also the random walk theory, in which followers believe that market prices follow a completely random path up and down, without any influence being exerted on them by past price action, making it impossible to predict with any accuracy which direction the market will move at any point or indeed to what degree. However, as has been proven repeatedly, this is plainly incorrect, as patterns of all sorts manifest themselves daily, indeed hourly, and all that is required is to know what to look for. Risk/reward ratios are what a trader needs to know, and the basics of these were covered in the *Trading Oil And Gas Market FX Correlations* section earlier.

# Hedging

A perfect hedge means one in which no risk whatsoever is taken. As a corollary of this, it means that there will also be no reward. The perfect hedge would be, for instance, buying WTI crude oil and selling it simultaneously – clearly a pointless exercise. Instead, hedging in real trading terms involves off-setting some of the risks involved in a trade, either by reducing risk in a particularly position or by increasing reward for it, through other trades. In this sense, then, hedging is a method of dynamically managing the risk/reward profile for the trader, and the trader needs to know what the current correlations are in order to maximise reward and limit risk (see earlier sections on *Correlations*). More specifically, though, for oil trading, the following should always be looked at as first ports of call.

## Cross-Commodities Hedging

**Commodities differ from stocks or bonds in that they usually they have a major function in some industry or another.** For example, platinum is used extensively in the car industry (in catalytic converters) plus in laboratory equipment, electrical contacts and electrodes, resistance thermometers and dental equipment, in addition to being used as store of value. Silver, too, aside from its more limited use as a store of value, is widely used in solar panels and in the medical industry (silver nitrate solutions and its compounds are used in disinfectants and microbiocides). And gold, whilst used extensively as a store of value, has practical uses, especially in the computer industry.

This is **qualitatively different from currencies, equities and bonds, which have no industrial use but do generate cashflows (in terms of relative interest rates, dividends, coupon or the principal) that commodities do not. Indeed, the only return that commodities give the investor is when their prices move up or down** (if long or short).

The main **idea behind the gold-oil relation is the one which suggests that prices of crude oil partly account for inflation, which has been particularly evident when the oil price has fallen a long way fast and inflation has tumbled around the globe with it.** More specifically, increases in the price of oil result in increased prices of gasoline which is derived from oil, and if gasoline is more expensive then it is more costly to transport goods and their prices consequently increase. Of course, the reverse is true, as the declining trend in global inflation has shown. The second part of this idea is that demand for precious metals (notably gold) tends to increase as inflation rises (as an **inflation hedge**) but it is also true that in times of higher perceived global economic risk (as has been seen with the falling price of oil raising questions over the North American shale industry and over the prospects for major oil and gas producers) demand for gold holds its own (**risk hedge**), and this is what the markets have seen since the latest oil price decline.

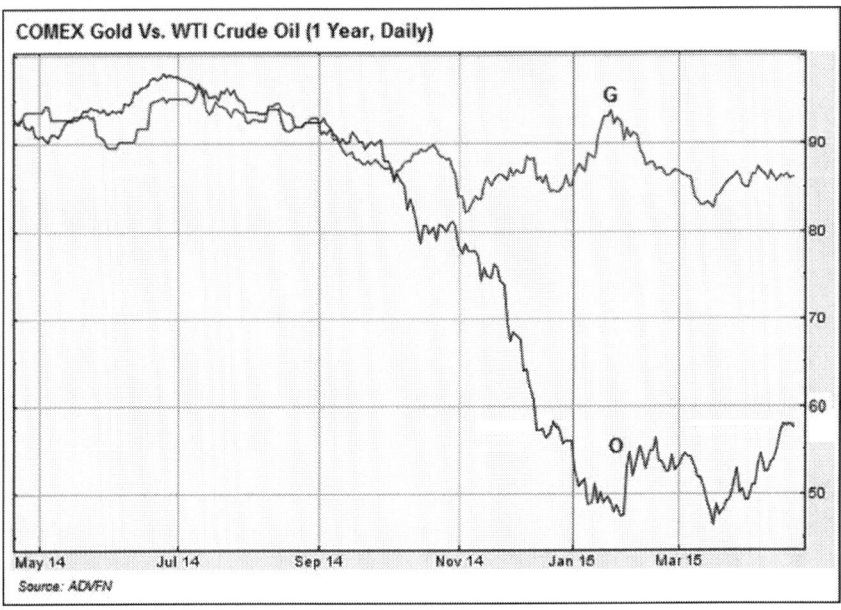

*[Chart Key:*
*G = Comex Gold price*
*O = WTO Oil Price]*

Consequently, as can be seen from the above chart, at the point when the Saudis said that they did not care whether the oil price went to even USD20/bbl, buying gold would have offset losses in a long crude oil position, and these discrepancies (risk hedge outweighing inflation hedge) have appeared in times of market uncertainty many times before as the chart below illustrates.

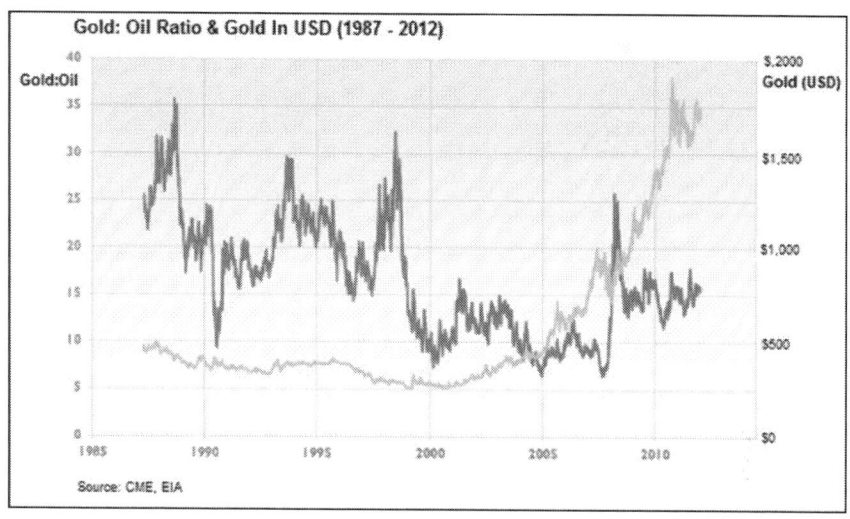

## Cross-Asset Class Hedging

Going on the basis of having taken out a long crude position just as it began its major decline, the choices so far examined in this section have been:

1. Get out of the position once it has hit the level at which a stop-loss order should have been triggered (it should have been put on at the same time as the entry order to buy) or if an order had not been left then manually execute a sell order to nullify the long position.
2. Buy gold to at least offset the loss on the long oil position.

However, as highlighted in the earlier sections on *Correlations*, if a trader (for reasons of long-term expectations) does not want to unwind the long oil position then there are other ways not just to mitigate losses but to turn exponential profits on a net/net trading basis.

For example, as mentioned earlier, given the relationship between oil and the USD, going long the USD would have yielded huge profits at the same time as the oil price long was losing money, as shown below.

## Oil Price Action (2 Years, Daily)

[Chart Key:

A and B = Exploration at the edges of the Permian shale and experimentation with new technologies revealed that the aerial acreage of shale was likely double what was initially thought and that much more oil could be squeezed from the shale formations

C = Announcement by Prince Turki Al Faisal, an influential Saudi Arabian royal and businessman, that the Gulf Kingdom planned to dramatically increase its oil production capacity (from 12.5 million barrels a day to 15 million barrels a day) by 2020

*D = Private meetings between Saudi officials and other senior figures in the global oil industry in New York in October 2014 (which were publically reported shortly after) in which the Saudis appeared to reveal that the Kingdom – far from looking to keep prices high (as had been the normal inclination of OPEC for many years, in order to boost the prosperity of OPEC member states) – was willing to tolerate oil prices as low as USD80-USD90/bbl for a period of 1-2 years (through increasing production)*

*E = In December 2014, Saudi Oil Minister Ali Al Naimi openly stated in an interview on CNN that far from contemplating any cuts in production to support the oil price: "We are going to continue to produce what we are producing, we are going to continue to welcome additional production if customers come and ask for it."*

*F = In the same month, Al Naimi added that Saudi Arabia did not care whether the oil price fell to even as low as USD20/bbl; his exact words were: "Whether it [oil] goes down to USD20, USD40, USD50, USD60, it is irrelevant." This was unusually straightforward for a Middle Eastern oil minister and as such should have been acted on immediately.*

*G = Technical analysis was also confirming the same position, breaking through a long-established support level at USD91.50, and the RSI levels were consistently near overbought levels]*

If a trader had gone long at the 91.50 level, thinking that the longstanding support level would hold or, once broken, would be revisited again swiftly, only to find that the oil price was falling (and gapping) quickly, so much so that he had not been able to get out of the position around his theoretical stop-loss level (which is why, again, putting on the stop-loss order at the same time as taking out the entry point trade is vital to long-term success) then he could have taken out a long USD trade to mitigate against the oil position's losses, either through a long USD Index trade, as shown below:

or through going long the USD against another currency, preferably one which would be especially prone to a falling oil price trend, such as the CAD:

## USDCAD Price Action Over Same Period As Oil Price Fall

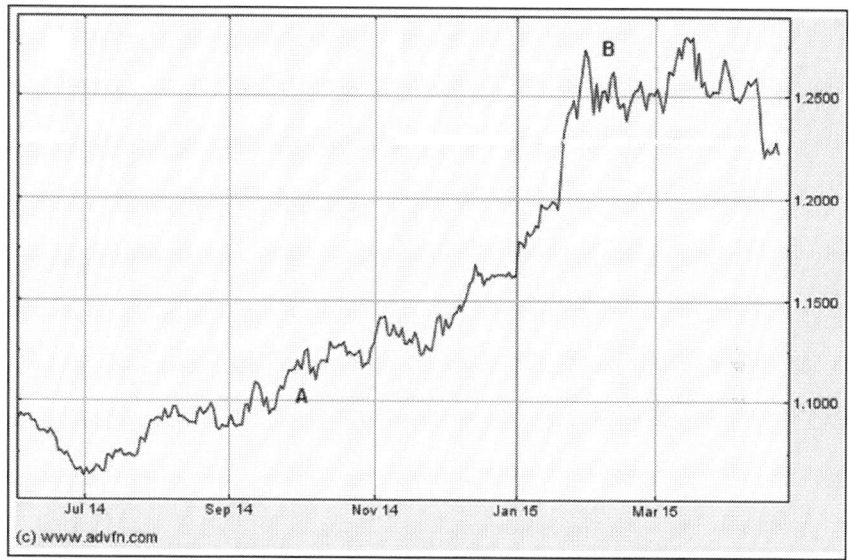

*[Chart Key:*
*A = Buy USDCAD*
*B = Sell USDCAD]*

Overall, using the same incremental increases in position that were used in the Oil Trade (i.e. as every major resistance point was breached) the trading would have looked as follows:

**USDCAD 6 Years Daily To Show Previous Resistance Levels**

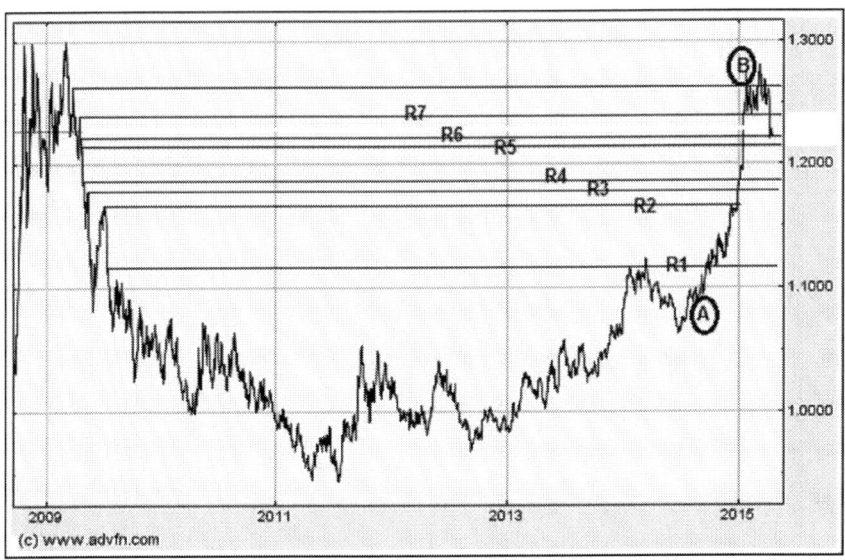

(c) www.advfn.com

**Long USDCAD Trade (hedging bad Long Oil Trade, GBP10pp trade to match oil trade amount and GBP10pp incremental additional buys as resistance levels break) =**

*A: Entry trade buy GBP10pp @ 1.1070, stop loss buy back @ 1.1055 (support level)*
*R1: Buy GBP10pp @ 1.1170*
*R2: Buy GBP10pp @ 1.1660*
*R3: Buy GBP10pp @ 1.1860*
*R4: Buy GBP10pp @ 1.1910*
*R5: Buy GBP10pp @ 1.2140*
*R6: Buy GBP10pp @ 1.2210*
*R7: Buy GBP10pp @ 1.2395*
*B: Exit trade sell all @ 1.2720, cancel trailing stop loss orders*

**Profit = GBP62,425**

Alternatively, using the macroeconomic correlations discussed earlier in the *Correlations* section, a trader could have gone long of equities markets that looked particularly likely to benefit from lower oil prices; that is, those with a high manufacturing base and a heavy exports-oriented economy, while not being a major energy producer itself (and thus not subject to the oil price downside from that perspective).

## Summary on Hedging

If one asset is going down another one is likely to be going up at the same time in direct proportion, so a trader needs to think laterally about all asset markets when he has a position, allowing him to get out of virtually any bad trade that he has made or to optimise profits on a good one.

Preferably, as discussed elsewhere, he should know all of the possible trading options available to him across as many asset markets as possible before he enters into the trade in the first place.

# Options

**An option is the right, but not the obligation, to buy or sell an asset at a particular price (the exercise price) on or before a specific future date (the exercise date).**

The two most common types of option are called an **American style option** (which can be exercised at any point up to the option expiration date) and a **European style option** (which can only be exercised on the specific exercise date).

For the more 'exotic' **Asian options** the payoff is determined by the average underlying price over some pre-set period of time, conceptually different from both the American and European option types in which in both cases the payoff of the option contract depends on the price of the underlying instrument at exercise.

An **option to buy an asset is a 'call' option and an option to sell one is a 'put' option, and any type of option can be bought or sold.** If an option is sold by the trader then he will receive a premium from the buyer (like an insurance premium), however, he is obligated as the seller to pay out to the buyer in the event that the option is exercised (and these payouts can be enormous, depending on how the option has moved).

**Options are extremely useful as hedging tools (this was their original purpose, as a type of insurance against unforeseen movements in asset prices) but, as with all financial assets, they can also be used for purely aggressive speculative purposes, and they can be extremely costly in the event that a trader is not a real expert in them. Even in the case of real experts, options positions can unravel very quickly and very expensively, as evidenced by the collapse of Long-Term Capital Management, which was founded by the people who created the modern options pricing model in the first place.**

In a currency option, then – say EURUSD – if a trader bought a EURUSD call then he would be buying the right (but not the obligation) to buy EUR and sell USD, and if he bought a EURUSD put then he would be buying the right (but not the obligation) to sell EUR and buy USD. And vice-versa if the trader was selling a call or put – he has a liability then to meet the obligation implied in the option if the buyer decides to exercise it.

One thing that it is useful to be aware of in the options market is that the premium paid to buy an option is a reflection both of the exercise price of the option (and whether it is currently in profit, ITM or out of profit, OTM, see above) and also the volatility of the market for the currency pair.

In the EURUSD example, if **the player had gone long EUR short USD at 1.0600 and the position had started to go against him almost from the off, the near-perfect hedge would have been to buy a EURUSD put (the right but not the obligation to sell EUR and buy USD) at a strike price of 1.0600** although the price would have to be adjusted slightly to take into account the premium that the player would have paid to the seller of the option.

He could, conversely, have banked money in advance if he had sold a EURUSD call option (giving someone the right but not the obligation to buy EUR from the player, therefore the player is selling them and buying USD) also at 1.0600.

There are more interesting ways to actually make money from options, of course, by locking in certain profit zones through a combination of buying and selling calls and puts at different prices, taken together with different hedging techniques, but for the retail trader it is not especially something they should be considering, certainly not in the first few phases of his development.

A key part of why more investors in general are now looking at options (and futures) investment than were before the new swathe of market regulations (Basel III, Mifid, Dodd-Frank etc), of course, is that they appear to fall outside the confusion of precisely what will and will not be actively managed within the scope of the new FX regulatory environment.

For example, one key idea was that the traditionally bilaterally-traded over-the-counter (OTC) FX derivatives markets would be migrated into a mandatory electronically-executed environment, all under the auspices of central counterparties (CCPs) that act as middlemen between the trading parties and the central clearinghouses. Moreover, participants would be obliged to post initial and variation margin to the CCPs on a daily or intra-day basis, so the need for easily accessible capital to enable such trading would also increase dramatically.

However, timing remains a problem for the futures markets, given that the dates of the contracts are much more specific than those of spot and forward outright contracts, which are completely flexible, and liquidity is also a problem for the futures markets, which are very small compared to the global FX markets.

The massive risk in writing options was highlighted in the Nick Leeson case. Nick Leeson was in charge of both Barings Bank's front office dealing operations on the Singapore International Monetary Exchange (SIMEX) and its back-office function so that when a trade went wrong at the front end he personally could simply rubber-stamp it at the back end, and he continued to do so until he lost Barings around GBP830 million, bringing the bank down in the process (this being a reminder of over-confidence in one's abilities).

In order to cover his mounting trading losses he decided to write vast numbers of options, essentially betting on the Nikkei stock market rising. He had pocketed millions of dollars in 'insurance options' from others and all was looking good as Japan boomed, until the Kobe earthquake hit Japan in January 1995, whereupon the Nikkei fell like a stone and his customers wanted their insurance payments back (thus illustrating that markets are not always predictable).

In sum, it is wise to be very careful indeed when thinking about using options.

# Technical Analysis

## Candlesticks

For those readers who bought my first book – *Everything You Need To Know About Making Serious Money Trading The Financial Markets* – you may wish to skip this section as it is largely a reiteration of what can be found in that book; unless, of course, you have been losing money, in which case it would probably bear reading again.

The **candlestick method of charting is particularly useful as it not only shows simply whether the market has largely bought the base currency (typically shown in green or white) or sold it (typically shown in red or black) but also how strong these buys or sells were (indicated by the length of the lines above each candle, 'wick', for buying or below, 'shadow', for selling).**

**Candlestick Structure**

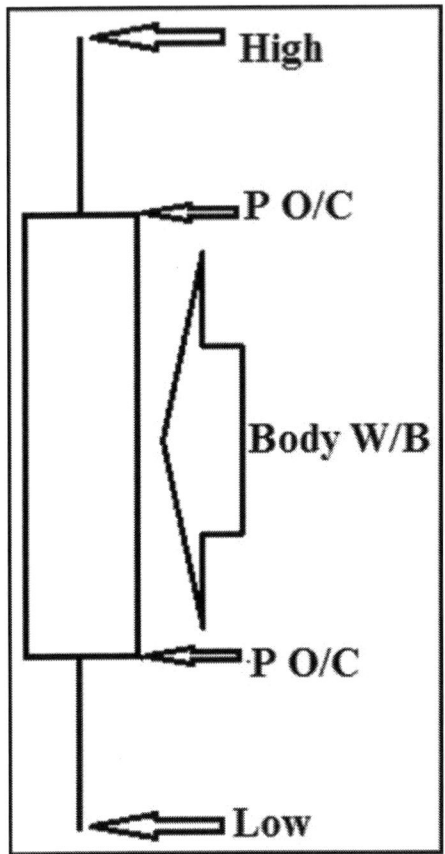

[Chart Key:

High = Highest price during trading time period

P O/C = Trading time period open or close price

Body W/B = Real body is white (or green) if currency closed higher over the trading period or black (or red) if it closed lower

P O/C = Trading time period open or close price

Low = Lowest price during trading time period]

If a market is undecided as to where it views the direction of a pair then the candlestick will have no substantial body, wick or shadow ('**doji**'), reflecting that the price closed the day where it opened and that neither buyers ('bulls') nor sellers ('bears') prevailed in moving the pair their way over the course of the trading hours.

A similar inference can be taken from the 'Spinning Top' pattern, although not to quite the same degree, as some intra-day movement will have taken place. In either event, both can be viewed as **marking possibly the end of the previous trend**, as it has run out of steam. These patterns make ideal places to enter new trades or exit existing ones.

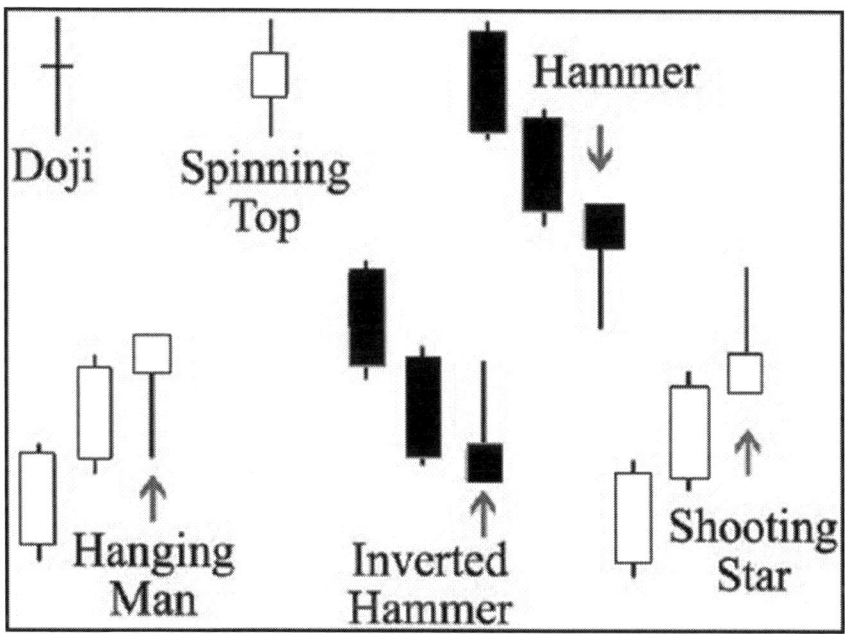

The 'Hammer' pattern appears after a previous move to the downside and indicates that a move to the upside is on the cards. The long shadow shows that, despite it trading substantially lower during the day, the weight of selling was not sufficient for it to stay at depressed trading levels. Consequently, the inference is that major buyers have stepped in at these levels and may well continue buying overnight or as the new Western trading period properly commences.

The same can be said for the 'Inverted Hammer', although to a lesser degree, as although buyers have stepped into the market, they have failed on this occasion to reverse the downtrend entirely.

Conversely, the 'Shooting Star' should be read as a sign that a move to the downside is on the cards, after a previous move to the upside, with bulls having failed to continue to push the pair higher and substantial bears having now entered the market.

The same can be said for the 'Hanging Man' although to a lesser degree, as although sellers have stepped into the market, they have failed on this occasion to reverse the uptrend entirely.

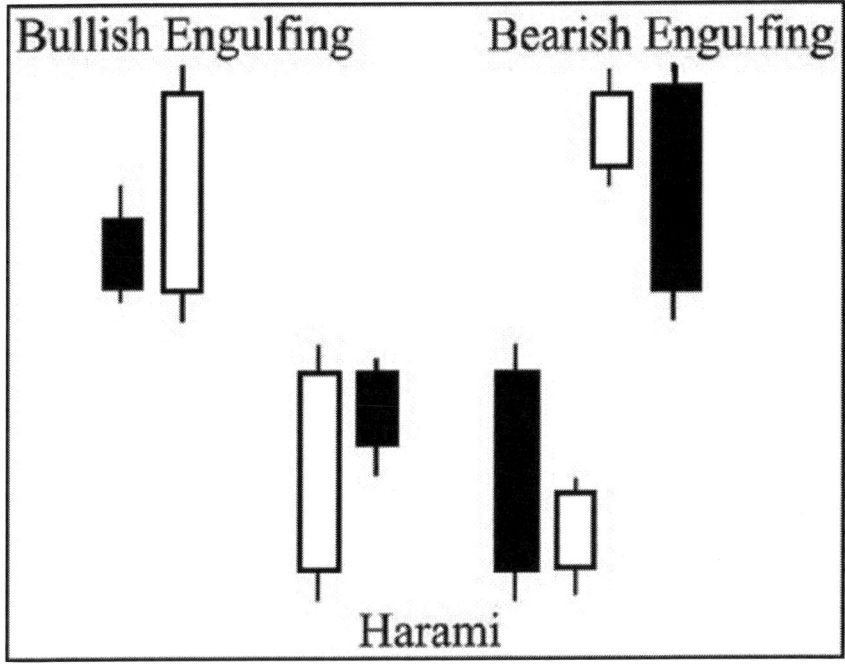

A 'Bullish Engulfing' pattern is a clear indication that the signs of reversal of a previous trend (either through a Shooting Star or Hanging Man) have gained momentum, and the reverse is true of the 'Bearish Engulfing' pattern (either through the Hammer or Inverted Hammer).

The 'Harami' pattern, though, which can occur after a move either up or down, can be taken again as a sign of uncertain price follow-through and may mark the beginning of a change of trend direction.

## USDCAD (Historic Illustration Of Key Technical Analysis Patterns)

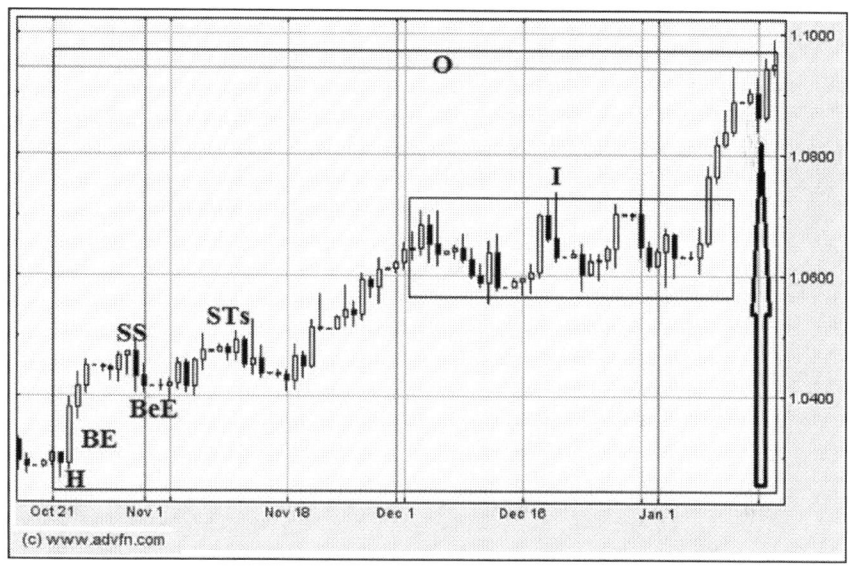

*[Chart Key:*
*H = Hammer*
*BE = Bullish engulfing*
*SS = Shooting star*
*BeE = Bearish engulfing*
*STs = Spinning tops*
*O = Overall uptrend*
*I = Indecision of the market]*

In all of the above cases, the **weight that should be attached to these patterns should be increased when additional confirmations are found.**

These can be where they occur at **major resistance and support levels, Fibonacci levels** (key mathematical ratios of an original number, representing a move up or down: 23.6%, 38.2%, 50% and 61.8%) or **Moving Average** levels (simply, each day's price added together and then divided by a certain number of days: 20, 50 and 100 are the most used), including selected oscillators.

In the above chart, for instance, aside from a few moves down (which fail to gather momentum, as indicated by the Spinning Top patterns) all of the significant moves have been to the upside (as indicated by the rolling Hammer patterns).

# Resistance And Support Levels

**Support levels** are established where the market has overwhelmingly bought the asset (or the base currency in currency trades) in the past, once it has been in a falling trend, and are found **below the current market price**, whilst **resistance levels** are established where the market has overwhelmingly sold the asset (or the base currency in currency trades) in the past, once it has been in a rising trend, and will be found **above the current market price**.

In other words, in chart terms, support levels can be found where selling turns to buying (denoted on candlestick charts, see below, as a red bar turning to green), whilst resistance levels can be found where buying turns to selling (denoted on candlestick stick charts as a green bar turning to red). R1 is the first resistance level and so on, whilst S1 is the first support level, with the current market price indicated as C.

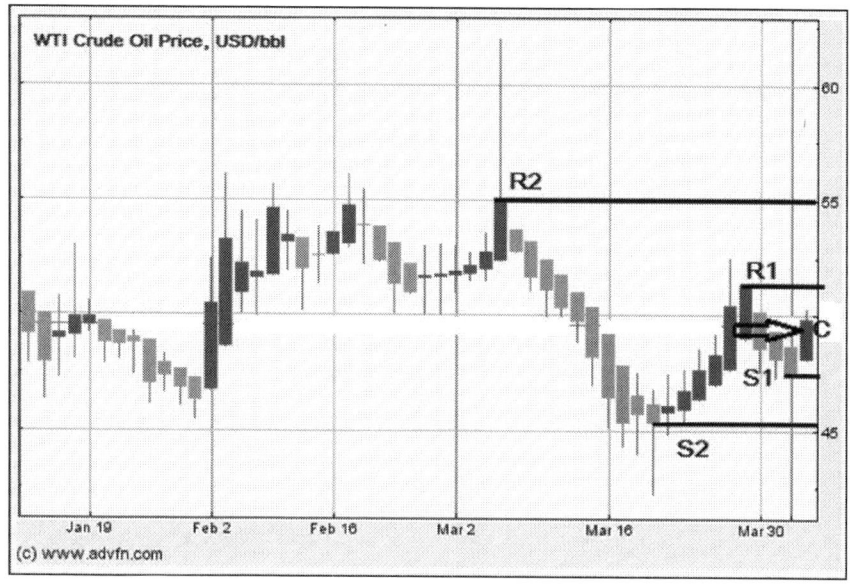

These levels should be the cornerstones of all serious trading activity, as they act (together with other confirmations, as discussed in the *Technical Analysis* section) as signals to buy or sell into a new position or to exit existing ones. It is important to know that the strength of support and resistance levels is increased when additional technical analysis confirmation factors are also present, and one of these is the RSI.

In general terms, the RSI shows the momentum of an asset's trading – in effect, the degree of market participation in its current price movement – and can act as a valuable pre-emptive indicator showing a potential reversal of trend.

For example, even if a pair appears to be rising quickly, if the RSI is showing that negative momentum is occurring then it might be time to look at the other indicators that signalled a long position and look to either exit an existing long or establish a new short.

Conversely, as shown in the chart below, there is a very notable shift upwards in RSI higher before the actual market price follows it.

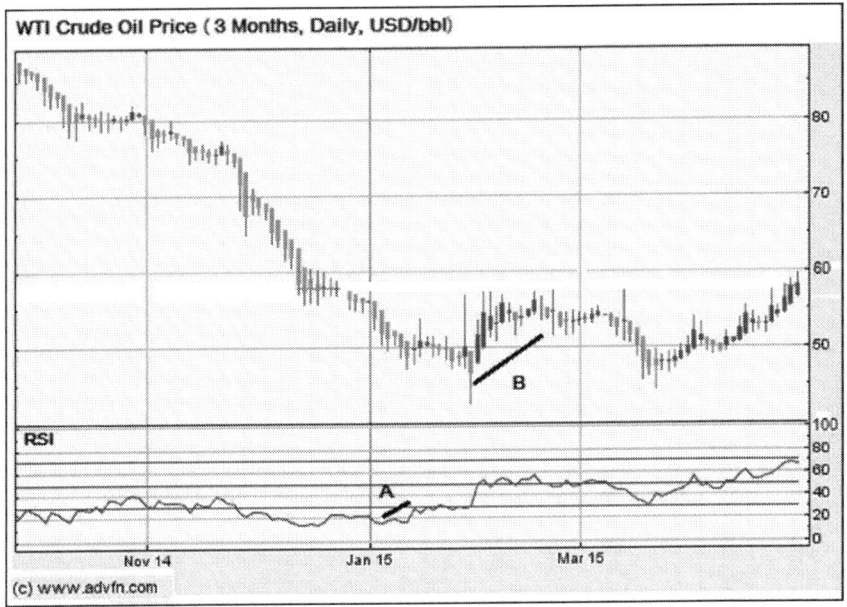

[Chart Key:

*A = RSI rises sharply higher, in advance of the price movement*

*B = Actual market price catches up with bullish momentum on RSI]*

**= RSI confirms upward trend before actual price turns higher**

More specifically, the RSI moves between a scale of 0 to 100, with 100 showing that every participant in the market is buying the base currency of a pair and 0 showing the opposite. **As a rule of thumb, any reading of 70 and above indicates that the pair is overbought, with a possible reversal on the cards, and any reading under 30 showing it is oversold and that the opposite is true.** This, together with the formations of usual double top/bottom patterns, can show up even before they do in the actual price movement ('Divergence').

Similarly, areas of support and resistance show up very clearly on RSI patterns, as shown below.

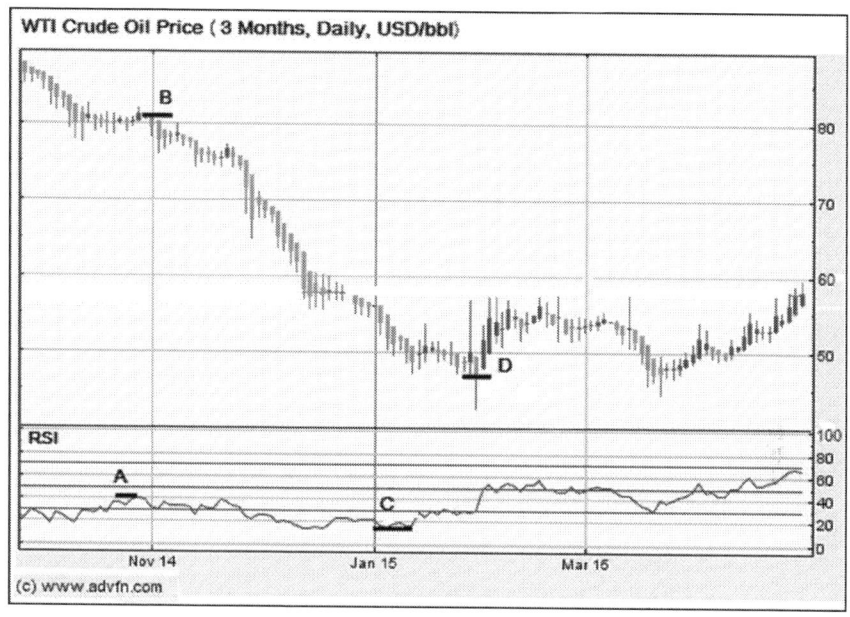

[Chart Key:

A = RSI shows genuine resistance level in the price, in advance

B = Market price subsequently reflects RSI action

C = RSI shows genuine support level in the price, in advance

D = Market price subsequently reflects RSI action]

As is evident from the above, RSI's principal use is not in already trending markets, in which it can be used as a confirmation of direction or as an early warning indicator of a change of direction (if above 70 or below 30) but rather in range-bound markets looking for direction.

Here, as shown above, it can act as a proxy for volume interest in particular positions, so that, for example, a sharp spike up in RSI in a market trading around the mid-level could be taken as an early signal of a bullish move and vice-versa.

# Fibonacci Levels

These are key mathematical ratios of an original number (price) representing a move up or down: **23.6%, 38.2%, 50% (not actually a Fibonacci ratio but most Fibonacci users include it anyhow), 61.8% and 100%.**

These can be overlaid on a chart, from the bottom of a trend to the top in a bullish market or from the top of a trend to the bottom in a bearish one.

As mentioned earlier, they can often mark resistance and support levels, as shown below.

**WTI Crude Oil Fall And First Fibonacci Retracement (1 Year, Daily, USD/bbl)**

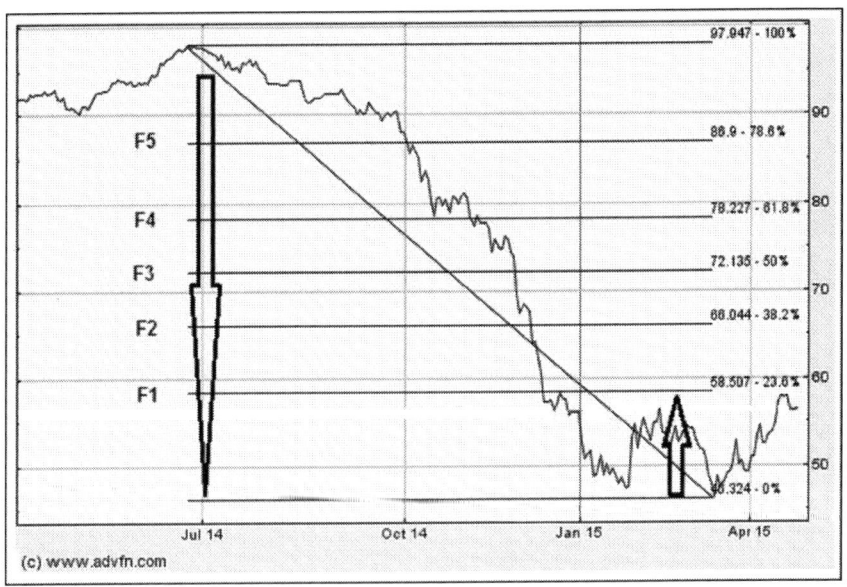

*[Chart Key:*
*F1 = Fibonacci level 1, 23.6%*
*F2 = Fibonacci level 2, 38.2%*
*F3 = Fibonacci level 3, 50.0%*

*F4 = Fibonacci level 2, 61.8%*
*F5 = Fibonacci level 3, 78.6%]*

It can be seen above that the first Fibonacci level has acted as a resistance level for the first potential move back up and, where these occur concomitant with the candlestick patterns as described above, they often point to a sustained move in whichever direction they break.

# Moving Averages

**These are particularly useful in determining short-term indications as to whether a market is set to continue in its current trend, reverse that trend or trade in a range.** As mentioned earlier, MAs are simply each day's price added together and then divided by a certain number of days.

As an additional confirmation (to established support and resistance levels, for instance), they offer a good idea of whether an asset is likely to break to the topside or the downside, as illustrated below.

## WTI Crude Oil Moving Averages Indicators (1 Year, Daily, USD/bbl)

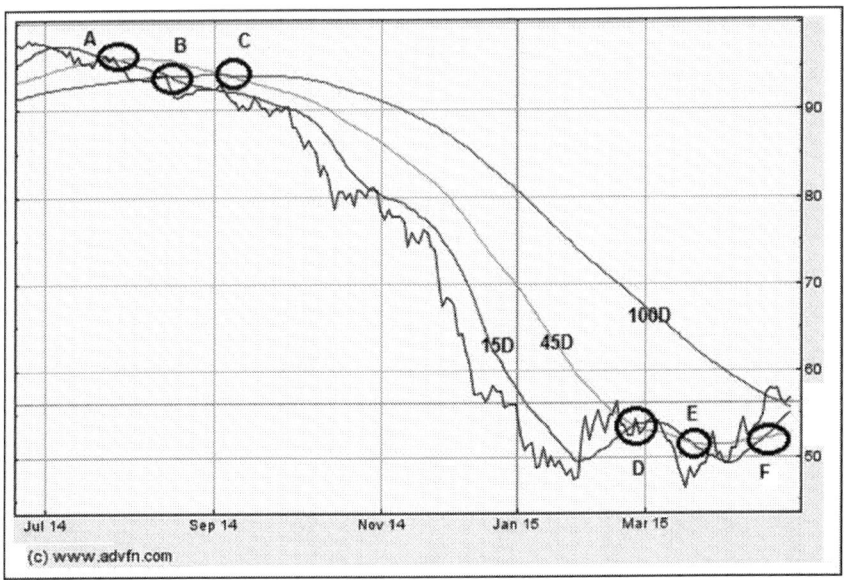

*[Chart Key =*
*15D = 15 day simple moving average (MA15)*
*45D = 45 day simple moving average (MA45)*
*100D = 100 day simple moving average (MA100)*
*A = MA15 down through MA45 = SELL*
*B = MA15 down through MA100 = SELL*
*C = MA45 down through MA100 = SELL*
*D = MA15 up through MA45 = BUY*
*E = MA15 down through MA45 = SELL*
*F = MA15 up through MA45 = BUY]*

**Broadly speaking, as shown above, if a shorter-term MA breaks through a longer-term MA then the asset is likely to trade in whichever direction that break has occurred.** The bigger the time period difference of the two MAs (in the above case, MA15 and MA100) then the more decisive that move will be.

**MAs are also a vital part of determining the momentum of a price movement, in its application with the 3/10 Oscillator or the 10/30 Oscillator.** These are simple indicators constructed by subtracting the longer Exponential Moving Average (in the above examples, either the 10 day or 30 day, respectively) periods from the shorter Exponential Moving Average (in the above examples, either the 3 day or 10 day, respectively). If these do not appear on a charting package then they can be manually replicated with the MACD by setting the short term parameter to 3, the long term parameter to 10 and the smoothing parameter to 1.

## WTI Crude Oil Price And Oscillator Indicator (1 Year, Daily, USD/bbl)

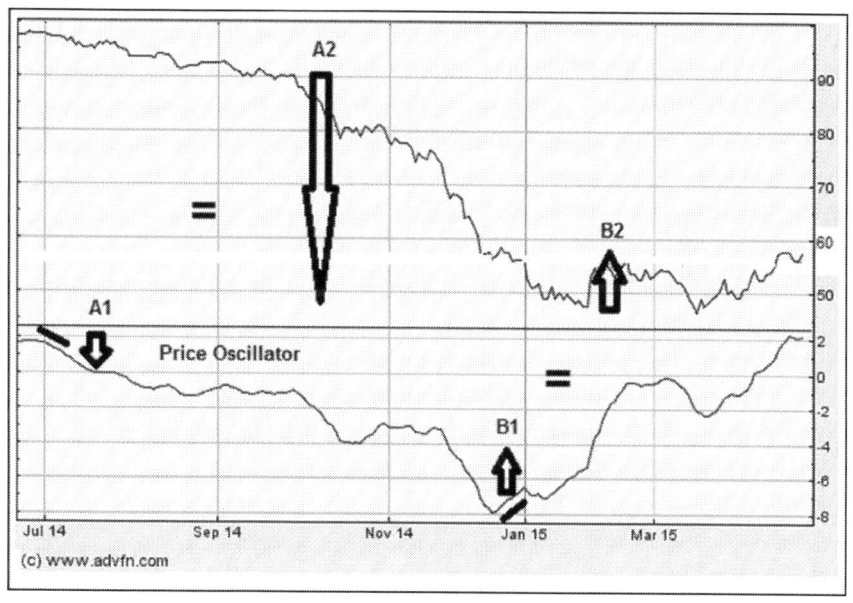

[Chart Key:

A1 and A2 = Sharp selling indication from price oscillator (A1) predicts sharp fall in oil price (A2)

B1 and B2 = Sharp reversal indication from price oscillator (B1) predicts rise in oil price (B2)]

The concept underlying this indicator (similar in theory to the RSI) is that if a price move up or down and is expected to be sustained then it would be anticipated that, along with a range of higher highs (for an upmove) or lower lows (for a downmove), the momentum (or force) behind each of these would also be sustained. If not, questions should be asked about whether the move can have the strength to continue.

# Relative Strength Index (RSI)

RSI is another extremely useful oscillator indicator. **In general terms, the RSI shows the momentum of an asset's trading – in effect, the degree of market participation in its current price movement – and can act as a valuable pre-emptive indicator showing a potential reversal of trend.**

For example, even if an asset appears to be rising quickly, if the RSI is showing that negative momentum is occurring then it might be time to look at the other indicators that signalled a long position and look to either exit an existing long or establish a new short.

Conversely, as shown in the chart below, there is a very notable shift upwards in RSI higher before the actual market price follows it.

## EURUSD Historical With RSI Pre-Empting Change Of Trend

*= RSI confirms upward trend before actual price turns higher*

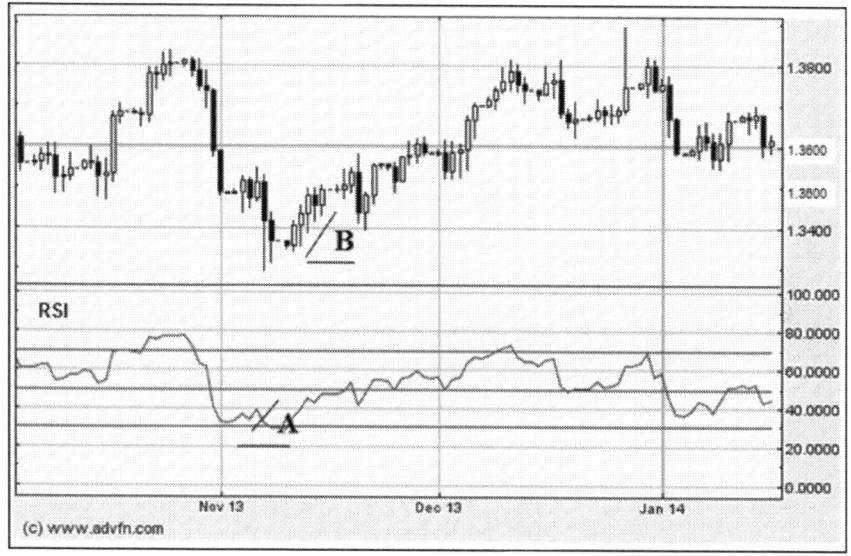

[Chart Key:

*A = RSI rises sharply higher, in advance of the price movement*

*B = Actual market price catches up with bullish momentum on RSI]*

More specifically, the RSI moves between a scale of 0 to 100, with 100 showing that every participant in the market is buying the base currency of a pair and 0 showing the opposite. **As a rule of thumb, any reading of 70 and above indicates that the pair is overbought, with a possible reversal on the cards, and any reading under 30 showing it is oversold and that the opposite is true.** This, together with the formations of usual double top/bottom patterns, can show up even before they do in the actual price movement ('Divergence').

Similarly, areas of support and resistance show up very clearly on RSI patterns, as shown below.

## WTI Crude Oil Price With RSI Pre-Empting Tops And Bottoms

*= RSI confirms topping out and bottoming out before reflection in market price*

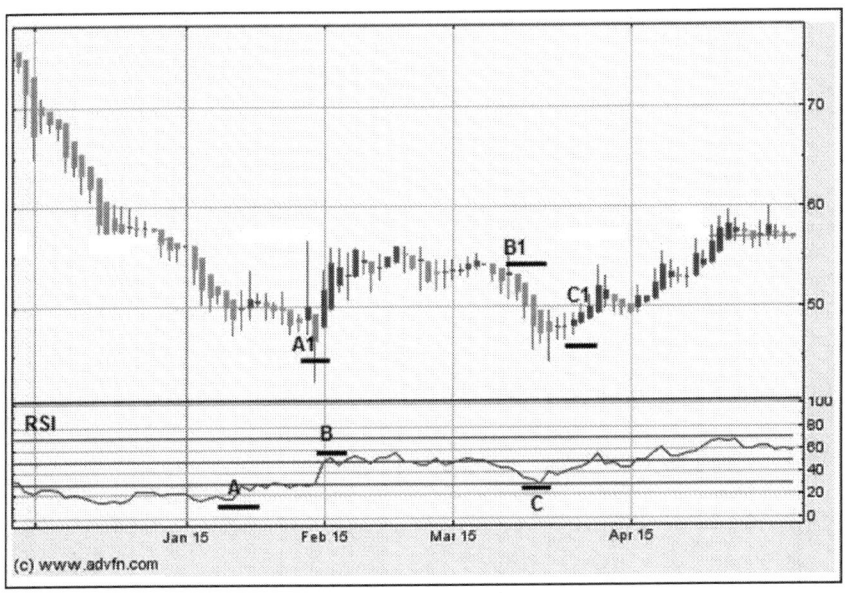

[Chart Key:

A = RSI shows genuine support level in the price, in advance of price move (A1)

B = RSI shows genuine resistance level in the price, in advance of price move (B1)

C = RSI shows genuine rolling support level, in advance of price reflection (C1)]

As is evident from the above, RSI's principal use is not in already trending markets, in which it can be used as a confirmation of direction or as an early warning indicator of a change of direction (if above 70 or below 30) but rather in range-bound markets looking for direction.

Here, as shown above, it can act as a proxy for volume interest in particular positions, so that, for example, a sharp spike up in RSI in a market trading around the mid-level could be taken as an early signal of a bullish move and vice-versa.

# Bollinger Bands

Bollinger bands are plotted an equal distance either side of a simple moving average. The default settings on trading programmes use a 20 period simple moving average with the upper band (UB) plotted 2 standard deviations above the moving average and the lower band (LB) plotted 2 standard deviations below it.

In periods of low price volatility, these standard deviations become smaller (this process is called a 'squeeze' in Bollinger parlance) than in periods of high volatility and vice-versa (a 'bubble').

Given this, there is undoubtedly money to be made from anticipating/participating in such a breakout/breakdown to the existing bands.

## WTI Crude Oil Price With Bollinger Bands

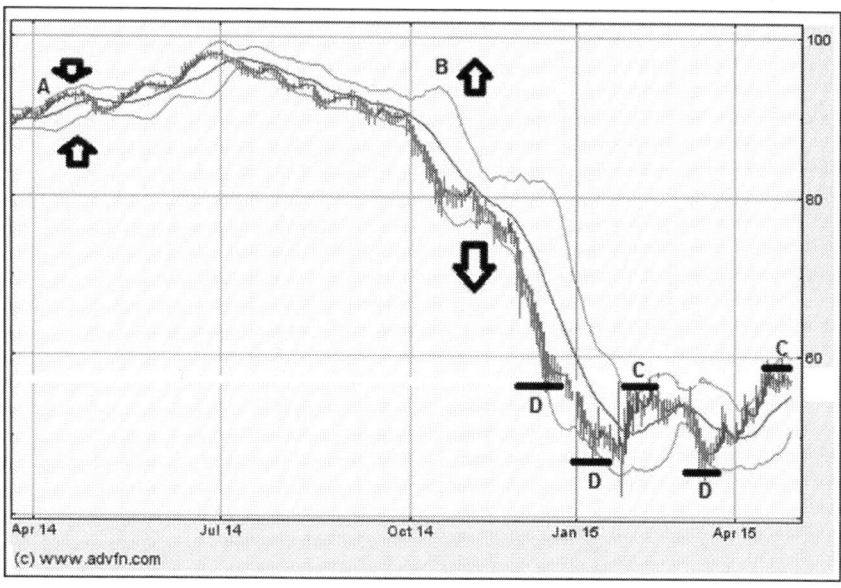

*[Chart Key:*
*A = Squeeze*
*B = Bubble*
*C = Upper band acts as resistance level*
*D = Lower band acts as support level]*

More appositely, it is better to use Bollinger bands together with other firmer indicators such as support and resistance levels, Fibonacci levels and so on, and to use them in such a way as to modify the results with what the Bollinger bands indicate about the probability of a move continuing/reversing.

**If the price is moving towards the top of a band then beware longs and if it is moving towards the bottom of a band then beware shorts;** however, taking investment cues from them alone is unwise.

# Elliott Wave Theory

Elliott Wave Theory is particularly useful as it shows major moves and minor ones, with the former likely to be caused by institutional investors (and well worth following, if they are not spoofs) and the latter likely to be caused by retail investors playing catch-up (normally a good time to start thinking about exiting a trade).

In its most basic form, Elliott Waves show that the market does not move in a completely chaotic fashion but rather is a product of patterns that repeat themselves over time. These patterns ('waves') define a trend, which can be the basis for predictive trading.

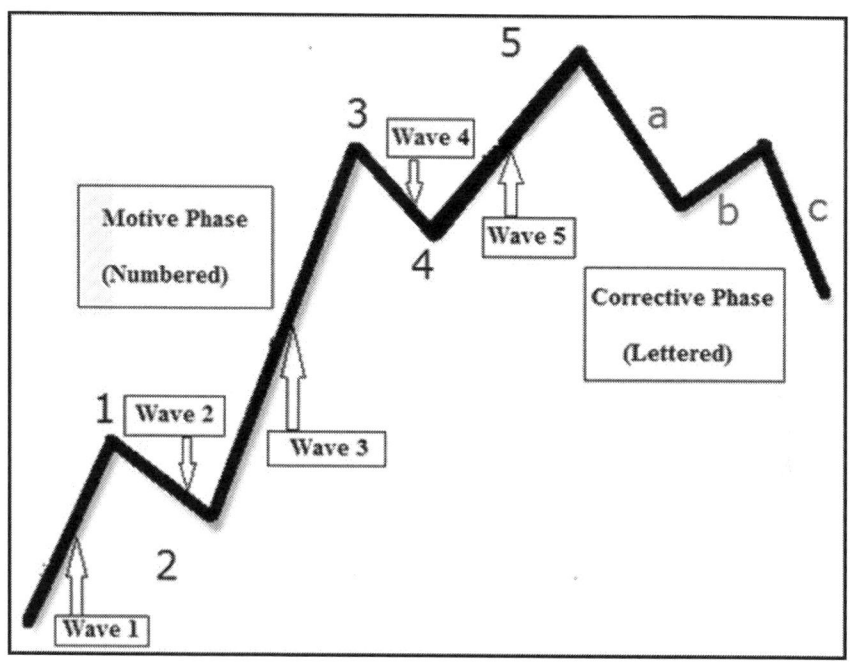

[*Chart Key:*
*See text below for 'Motive' and 'Corrective' definitions]*

More specifically, according to Elliott (Ralph Nelson Elliott who posited his theory in around 1934), a trending market moves in a **five-three wave** pattern, where the first five waves ('motive waves') move in the direction of the larger trend. Following the completion of the five waves in one direction, a larger corrective move takes place in three consecutive waves ('corrective waves'), as illustrated in the above chart.

Interestingly, **the patterns identified by Elliott occur across multiple time frames**: that is, a completed five wave sequence on a small time frame (5 minutes, for instance) may well be just the first wave of a longer temporal sequence (in a daily chart, for example) and so on. The **combination of Elliott Waves and Fibonacci ratios is particularly useful in trading into new positions or trading out of existing ones for a number of reasons**, outlined as follows: Fibonacci ratios are usually important levels of supply and demand (i.e., support and resistance).

**The motive and corrective levels are often measured by percentages of the previous wave length, with the most common levels being the Fibonacci ones of 38%, 50%, 61.8% and 100%**; timings with a distance of 13, 21, 34, 55, 89 and 144 periods should be particularly monitored (e.g., if a crucial reversal or an unfolding of a pattern on a daily chart is found then expect another crucial unfolding at the above daily points thereafter); a corrective move that follows a motive move from a significant low or high usually retraces 50% to 61.8% of the preceding impulse; wave 4 usually corrects as far as 38.2% of wave 3; given that wave 2 generally does not overlap the start of wave 1 (i.e., the 100% of it), the start of wave 1 is an ideal level to place stops; and the target of wave 5 can be calculated by multiplying the length of wave 1 by 3.236 (2 X 1.618).

# Continuation Patterns

**These patterns allow the trader not only to understand from where the price action and momentum has come but also to anticipate where and to what degree it is headed.** Thus, as these patterns are also watched by thousands of other traders around the globe, they allow a retail trader to obtain an ongoing record of the sentiment surrounding an asset at any given time and consequently allow the trader to manage his order placing better as well.

### Ascending And Descending Triangles

**Triangles basically allow the trader to gauge which of the myriad support and resistance levels on a chart are the ones he should be watching most carefully in determining false or genuine breakouts.**

An **ascending triangle** is formed by a combination of diagonal support and horizontal resistance, implying that the bulls are gaining the upper hand in the ongoing trading dynamic of the pair and buying at higher and higher levels, while the bears are merely trying to defend an established level of resistance.

**EURUSD Historical, Ascending Triangle**

[*Chart Key:*
*A = Horizontal resistance level*
*B = Inclining support*]

**Clearly, in the above example, the trader has advanced warning that the pair is more likely to break up through the resistance level than down through the support one.** Also, by anticipating the formation of the triangle the trader can gain/not lose further points, depending on his position, as assets often trend, consolidate and then re-trend.

In the case of a **descending triangle**, the bears are gaining strength and selling at lower and lower levels, while the bulls are merely trying to defend an established level of support.

## AUDUSD Historical, Descending Triangle

*[Chart Key:*
*A = Declining resistance*
*B = Horizontal support]*

**Given these two scenarios, it is easy to see that money can be made by riding the principal wave up or down respectively and also to see that triangles make the placement of stop loss orders relatively simple as well;** in the ascending triangle example, they would be placed just under the inclining support line at a level that accorded with a trader's risk/reward ratio for a rolling long position.

Conversely, in the descending triangle example, they would be placed at a point above the declining resistance level that accorded with a trader's risk/reward ratio for a rolling short.

In the cases of both ascending and descending triangles, **any true break (more than one spoof break-out) of its direction (up for descending triangles, down for ascending ones) should be taken seriously by traders to consider exiting trades made on the trend until that point (taking profit) and reversing positions.**

## Flags

**Flags and pennants generally represent a pause in trend and can be used either to take profits on a position going with that trend or to add to that trending position.**

The example below is of a downward trending USDJPY, which pauses for consolidation in a flag pattern, before resuming its downward trajectory. Often, the same number of pips in the second part of the downtrend (labelled 'Downtrend 2' in the chart, appositely enough) will occur as in the first part of the downtrend.

In the chart below, it seems on cursory glance that this is not the case. However, looking further into the distance and going on the basis of a longer-term trade, it becomes apparent that, in fact, the real second wave (or you could term it 'Downtrend 2, Part 2) makes up the entire pips expected as a result of Downtrend 1.

## USDJPY Historical, Flag In A Downtrend

(c) www.advfn.com

*[Chart Key:*
*A = Downtrend 1 = 723 pips*
*F = Flag*
*B = Downtrend 2 = 348 pips, OR DOES IT? See below]*

In fact, this flag and many similar presage a much sharper move down, as can be seen below.

## USDJPY Historical, Extended Continuation In A Downtrend

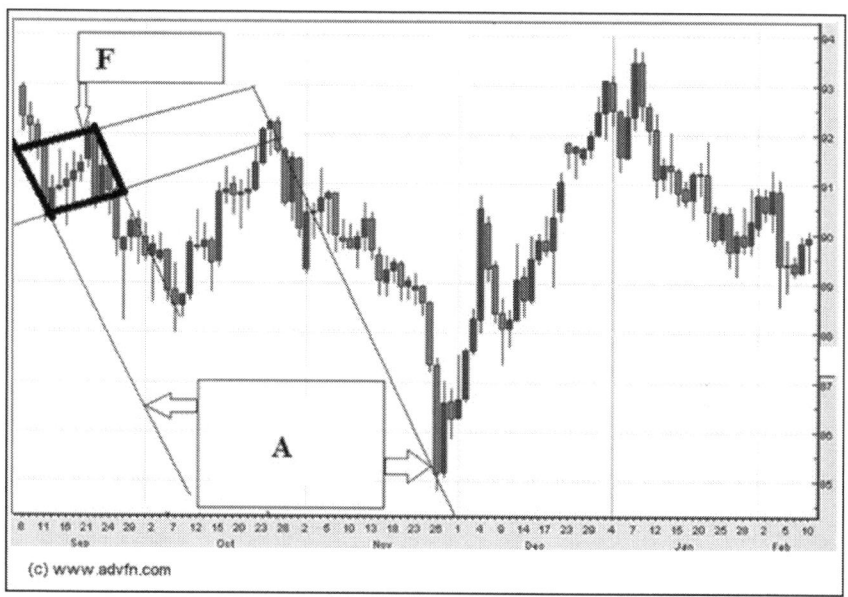

*[Chart Key:*
*F = Flag from previous chart*
*A = Logical conclusion of the original downtrend 1 = 700 pips had the trade*
*been stuck with]*

# Double Top/Bottom And
# Head And Shoulders Patterns

Given that the market has a way of generally correcting any untoward excessive movements one way or another in asset prices over time, spotting a real reversal in a trend from just a mirage is a key to making money on a long-term basis. In this respect, there are a couple of other, more basic patterns that a trader should look out for.

A **Double Top is when prices stop rising at the same point twice in a short sequence of time,** as shown below. In order for a real reversal of trend to be indicated, the pair must break down through the key support level as indicated on the chart. This is sometimes the result of a major institution (like a central bank) or a major supply player in commodities (like Saudi Arabia) looking to effect an economic outcome (like a central bank halting the appreciation of a currency in order to make exports more attractive and boost economic growth numbers) or to influence an asset for geopolitical ones (like Saudi Arabia looking to push the price of oil so low that the budding shale energy industry threat is halted in its tracks). This pattern can also be the result of major financial institutions looking to load the market in their favour (as discussed earlier in respect of hedge funds).

## GBPUSD Historical, Double Top

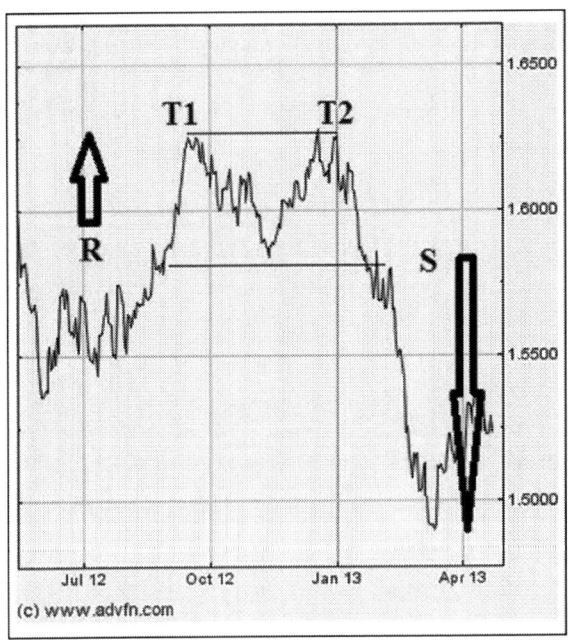

[Chart Key:
R = Rising trend
T1 = First top
T2 = Second (double) top

*S = Break below this double support level here implies downtrend]*

In the meantime, a head and shoulders pattern, as illustrated below, develops with the asset trending up and forming the left shoulder on a reversal. Then the market trends higher to form the head and falls back to the same support of the first shoulder to form the right shoulder. The neckline is thus the line connecting the troughs between the peaks. If it is broken, expect a downside move to occur.

## AUDUSD Historical, Head And Shoulders Trend Reversal Pattern

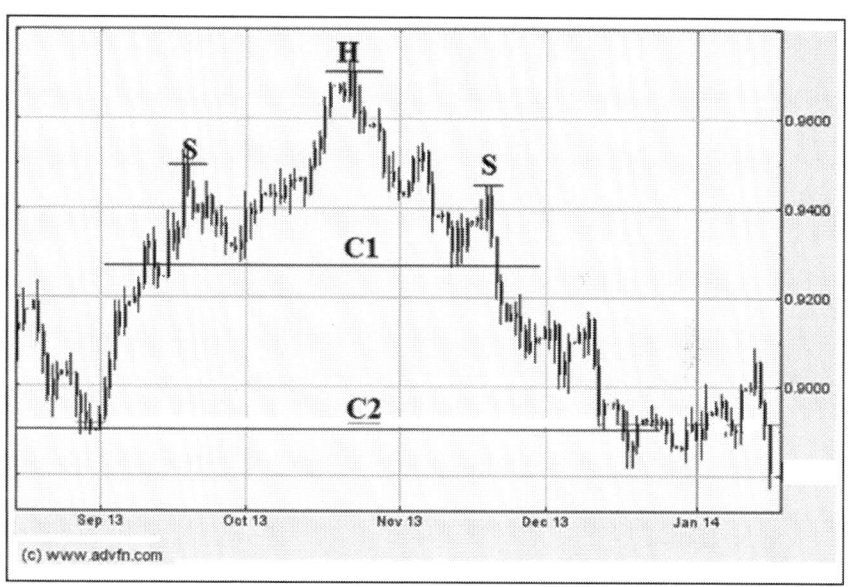

*[Chart Key:*
*S = Shoulder*
*H = Head*
*C1 = Confirmation of breakdown 1*
*C2 = Confirmation of further breakdown 2]*

# Technicals Vs Fundamentals
# For Oil Trading

In general terms, **on a day-to-day basis the technical factors of the oil market in and of itself matter less than they do in most notably the currency market (the equities market falls in between the two).** It is extremely common that intraday or intraweek trading in currencies will revolve around the key technical levels described in detail above (support and resistance, Fibonacci levels and in particular RSI) and that economic announcements from the countries whose currencies are a focus of trading at any particular point may play second fiddle to the technicals. This is not true generally for the oil market.

The reasons for this difference are:

1. That **the currency market is not in major part subject to the simple laws of supply and demand (except, of course, when there is a QE operation underway, in which the tendency will be for an extra supply of currency to tend towards a broadly weakening trend), whereas the oil market is. Consequently, data releases or major statements by major oil producers on oil supply and demand far outrank technical factors on the day in particular when they are due,** and the simple fact is that if oil supply figures (inventory numbers) are less than expected then the oil price will tend to rise quite sharply, depending on the disconnect between expectations and the actual data number.

2. The **forward guidance of major central banks – and states' major independent financial bodies (like the OBR in the UK for example) – on expected major data numbers is far more transparent and accurate than the guidance that comes from big oil producing states. Saudi Arabia, for**

**example, will just start to produce (or cut) its supply with no advance warning whatsoever.** Similarly, the US's Energy Information Administration's Weekly Petroleum Report will have no meaningful guidance in advance of its release, and even if there are rumours in the market about what the numbers will be (for oil inventory and gasoline inventory) then they will more than likely be way off the mark. Consequently, the weight of data releases or statements by major producers can completely override any technical trading considerations, and shorter-term technicals in the oil market are optimally employed during periods when oil numbers have already come out or are not due. They are also very effective at determining longer-term trends.

# Technicals And Fundamentals Will Align

The current great oil price fix, as highlighted earlier, is that which involves Saudi Arabia leading a massive sustained increase in global oil production in order to force oil prices lower with the aim of killing off the existential threat from nascent shale energy industry to both its status as the world's 'swing' producer of oil and, as a corollary of this, to its global geopolitical importance.

**The past few months has seen some success for it in realising this aim, with the global oil benchmark prices (Brent and WTI) having dropped by around 60% at one point** and then staying below that key level for some considerable time, so recent news from the Saudis (through its state oil and gas behemoth Saudi Aramco) that it is to direct the vast bulk of its spending over the next 10 years on boosting oil production might seem like overkill in its ongoing attempt to derail the nascent shale energy revolution, especially given the deleterious effect on its own budget as mentioned.

| Brent Oil Prices Required To Meet Various Fiscal Sustainability Thresholds ( US$/bbl) | | | | | | |
|---|---|---|---|---|---|---|
| | GS primary deficit breakeven (2015E production) | Debt / GDP | Price needed to keep Debt/GDP constant | | Price needed to reach 40% Debt/GDP ratio in 3 years | Reserves / Public Debt |
| | | | After 1 year | After 2 years | | |
| Kuwait | $60 | 11% | $63 | $69 | $64 | 102.2 |
| UAE | $64 | 12% | $71 | $86 | $38 | 17.0 |
| Qatar | $68 | 35% | $71 | $80 | $77 | 3.0 |
| Saudi | $83 | 3% | $85 | $88 | $79 | 35.8 |
| Russia | $101 | 10% | $104 | $108 | $92 | 2.9 |
| Algeria | $106 | 9% | $108 | $109 | $92 | 14.1 |
| Angola | $117 | 39% | $128 | $145 | $142 | 1.9 |
| Iraq | $126 | 31% | $131 | $136 | $133 | 1.3 |
| Iran | $133 | 11% | $139 | $141 | $98 | 3.3 |
| Nigeria | $144 | 10% | $158 | $182 | $129 | 6.6 |
| Libya | $185 | 5% | $204 | $230 | $180 | |

\* Reserves include SWF where applicable. Total production includes crude, NGLs and nonconventional oils.
*Source: IEA, IMF, World Bank, African Development Bank, Goldman Sachs*

In the wake of previous reductions, the US oil rig count in the first quarter of 2015 saw its biggest period-on-period fall since 1991 and, according to industry data, around one third of the 800 oil and gas projects (worth USD500 billion and totalling nearly 60 billion barrels of oil equivalent) scheduled for final investment decisions (FID) this year are 'unconventional' and thus especially vulnerable to the low oil pricing complex.

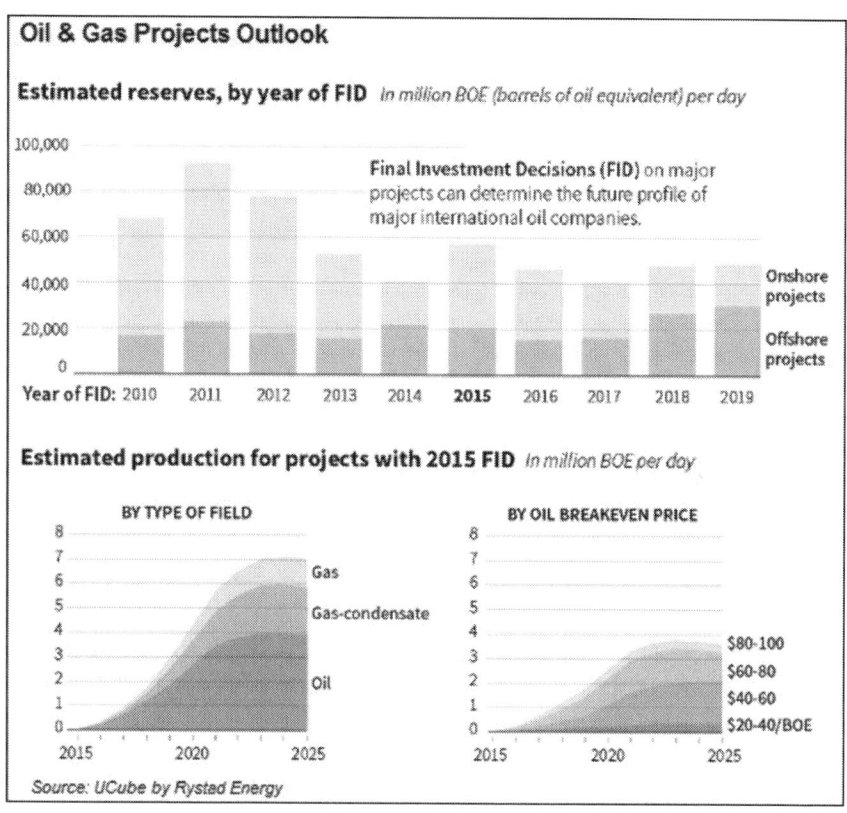

**Oil & Gas Projects Outlook**

**Estimated reserves, by year of FID** *In million BOE (barrels of oil equivalent) per day*

Final Investment Decisions (FID) on major projects can determine the future profile of major international oil companies.

Onshore projects

Offshore projects

**Estimated production for projects with 2015 FID** *In million BOE per day*

BY TYPE OF FIELD

Gas
Gas-condensate
Oil

BY OIL BREAKEVEN PRICE

$80-100
$60-80
$40-60
$20-40/BOE

Source: UCube by Rystad Energy

However, **despite non-OPEC producers having cut capex and idled rigs aggressively at the same time as demand has recovered strongly, the recent first price mini-rally break through to the USD60/bbl appears premature,** and should WTI remain near this level then US producers for one would eventually ramp up activity and complete wells, given improved returns with costs down by at least 20%, so negating the fundamental objective of Saudi's price squeeze in the first place.

Indeed, **even with the sustained higher production pressure from Saudi, the US rig curtailment so far has not been large enough to put its overall production on a persistent downward trend, given continued efficiency gains, signs of high grading and an elevated well backlog which could add at least 250,000 barrels per day of production when redeployed.** In fact, many serious oil market players project OECD inventories to only gradually draw in 2016, despite rising Chinese Strategic Petroleum Reserve builds and non-OPEC production declining outside the US, and the longer this price decline takes to materialise, the greater the upside risks to the market's already projected high inventories into 2016, especially in the US.

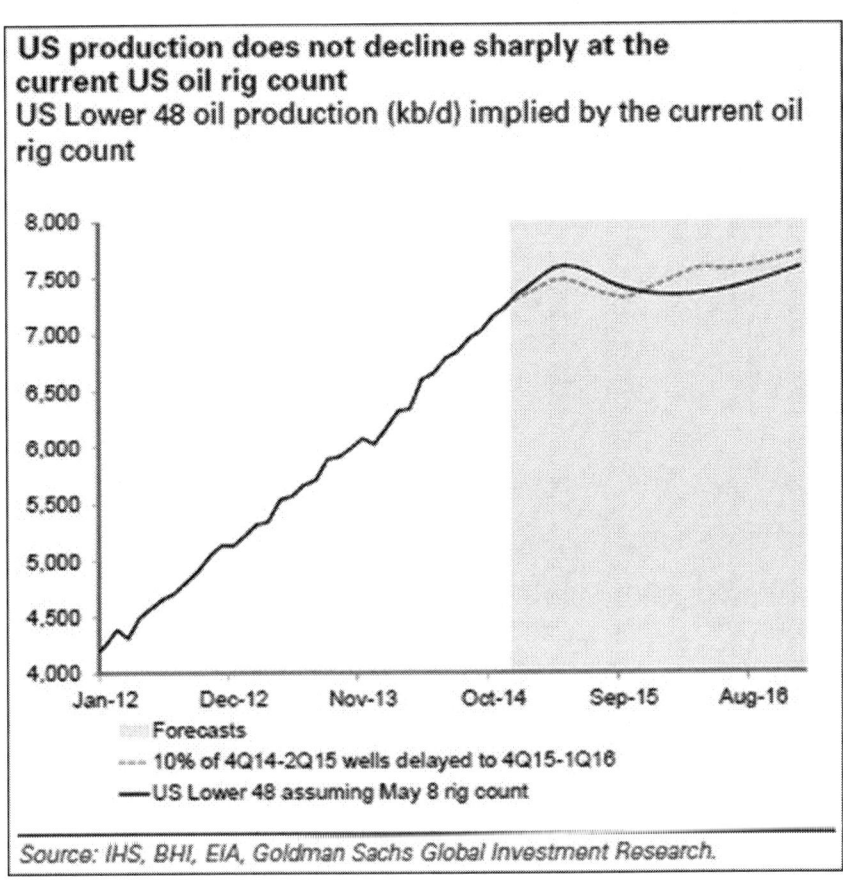

**US production does not decline sharply at the current US oil rig count**
US Lower 48 oil production (kb/d) implied by the current oil rig count

Forecasts
- - - 10% of 4Q14-2Q15 wells delayed to 4Q15-1Q16
——US Lower 48 assuming May 8 rig count

*Source: IHS, BHI, EIA, Goldman Sachs Global Investment Research.*

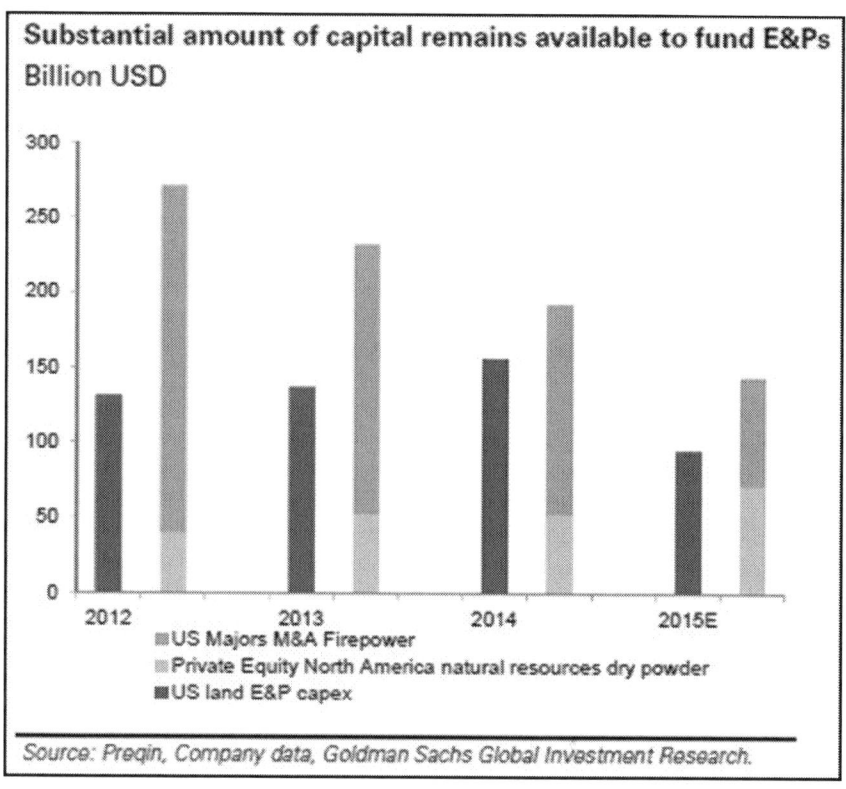

**Substantial amount of capital remains available to fund E&Ps**
Billion USD

- US Majors M&A Firepower
- Private Equity North America natural resources dry powder
- US land E&P capex

*Source: Preqin, Company data, Goldman Sachs Global Investment Research.*

According to Aramco's figures, global oil demand is expected to rise to 111 million bbl/d in 2040 from around 93 million bbl/d currently, and a recent OPEC report highlighted that although oil is likely to stay under the USD100/bbl figure at least until 2025, crucially within that headline figure there may be extended periods during that timeframe where it trades at or above the USD60/bbl, based on current production plans by its major producers, such as Saudi.

These, though, have not taken into account the potential extra production that Saudi announced at the beginning of May 2015. This could be considerable and magnified by the fact that Aramco is also to invest in increasing gas production so that an even greater percentage of its oil can go to export rather than be consumed in the domestic power market. In this respect, there are plans to bring online the expansion of the Shaybah oilfield to 1 million bbl/d in

April 2016, earlier than the previous official guidance of end-2016/early 2017, although no mention has been made of Khurais. The Wasit gas plant is also expected to go online this year, the Fadhili gas plant by 2019 and Midyan by the end of 2016, with the three gas plants projected to add more than 5 billion standard cubic feet per day (scfd) of non-associated gas processing capacity (11.3 billion scfd of raw gas was processed by Aramco last year, a 3% increase from 2013). This will further augment the output from the eight new oil and gas fields in the east of the country that Aramco discovered last year – five new gas fields in Abu Ali, Faras, Amjad, Badi and Faris, two oil fields in Sadawi and Naqa, and an oil and gas field named Qadqad.

This new supply should be significant, if the results of 2014's investment programme are any guide, with the oil giant pumping an average of 9.5 million bbl/d last year, with over 62% of its exports going to Asia and, according to the firm, both its oil and gas reserves hitting all-time record highs, at 261.1 billion barrels for oil and 294 trillion cubic feet for gas. The necessity for covering as much of the domestic power demand as possible with gas was also highlighted by the fact that actual crude oil exports were slightly lower last year at 2.544 billion barrels (or 6.7 million bbl/d), against 2.677 billion barrels (7.3 million bbl/d) in 2013, which again **underlines the fragility of the Kingdom's stymieing-shale strategy as it pans out in practice.**

Moreover, **although Aramco claims that last year's investment programme took its output capacity up to 12 million bbl/d, many questions remain over the veracity of these reserves numbers and those relating to its excess capacity,** with many serious market players believing that its excess capacity is nowhere near its often stated spare capacity of between 2-2.5 million bbl/d, with the capability to ramp up its production to about 12.5 million bbl/d in the event of unexpected disruptions elsewhere.

Scepticism over these figures has been supported by recent comments by Gulf officials at OPEC, which stated in the midst of

Iraqi supply fears that Saudi Arabia could ramp-up output by another 1 million bbl/d-1.3 million bbl/d in a best case scenario, adding that production of 11.5 million bbl/d is untested and could only be maintained for a very short period, if at all. Moreover, higher production for an extended period would be very difficult and would require producing heavy crudes.

In addition, it has been noted that the country's rising domestic consumption, notably to power its growing electricity generation networks and transport sector, has been eating into the country's crude export potential. Despite Saudi Arabia's heavy focus on developing its gas resources to support its crude export growth, as mentioned, it is expected that the slow development will be insufficient to offset rampant growth in demand for electricity leaving a heavy reliance on oil. Combined with growing electricity demand, Saudi Aramco's aggressive downstream expansion will put further pressure on domestic consumption in the coming years, and this will persist in progressively reducing the country's spare oil production capacity.

In sum, serious market players estimate Saudi's total liquids (oil and NGLs) capacity, including what's not being utilised, and not just on the OPEC line on spare capacity being 2.4 million bbl/d, as being 0.5 million bbl/d at most.

Once this attempted Saudi fix has run its course, then, traders will be back to playing the enduring financial markets' fix, as described in detail throughout the book.

# ABOUT THE AUTHOR

After graduating from Oxford University with BA (Hons) and MA (Hons) degrees, Simon Watkins worked for a number of years as a senior Forex trader and salesman, ultimately achieving the positions of **Director of Forex at Bank of Montreal and Head of Forex Institutional Sales for Credit Lyonnais.** He has since become a **financial journalist, being Head of Weekly Publications And Managing Editor and Chief Writer of Business Monitor International, Head of Global Fuel Oil Products for Platts, Global Managing Editor of Research for Renaissance Capital (Moscow)** and **Head of Developed Market Bond Analysis for Bond Radar.**

He has written extensively on Forex, equities, bonds and commodities for many publications, including: *The Financial Times, Euromoney, FT Capital Insights, FX-MM, CFO Insight, The Edge Middle East Finance, International Commerce Magazine, The Securities And Investment Review, Accountancy Magazine, The Emerging Markets Monitor, Asia Economic Alert, Latin America Economic Alert, Eastern Europe Economic Alert, Oil And Gas Middle East, European CEO, Global Finance*

*Magazine, World Finance Magazine, The Emerging Markets Report, FTSE Global Markets, VM Group Energy Monthly, VM Group Metals Monthly, Islamic Investor Magazine, Finance Europe, Finance Emerging Europe* and *CIMA Financial Management.*

In addition, he has worked as an investment consultant for major hedge funds in London, Moscow and the Middle East.

This is Simon's third book for ADVFN Books. Turn over for details of his first two.

**ALSO BY SIMON WATKINS**

# How to Make Big Money Trading in All Financial Conditions

The markets are going through a period of turbulence right now, but even in periods of low market volatility there's always some asset, somewhere in the world, that oscillates in price sufficiently to offer traders opportunities to make big money. The trick is to know what the asset is, to identify whether it's trading higher or lower than it should be and to have the skill, speed of thought and tenacity to take advantage of it.

In the follow up to his book *Everything You Need To Know About Making Serious Money Trading The Financial Markets*, Simon Watkins covers changing volatility patterns, risk-on/risk-off trading, how to find value in emerging markets and long-term global economic cycles. He outlines more fundamental principles that should guide your trades and trading methodologies to help you succeed.

Fully illustrated with detailed charts, the book shows how you can use technical analysis to make your decisions, how to manage your risk and how to take out hedge positions to offset possible losses.

# Everything You Need To Know About Making Serious Money Trading The Financial Markets

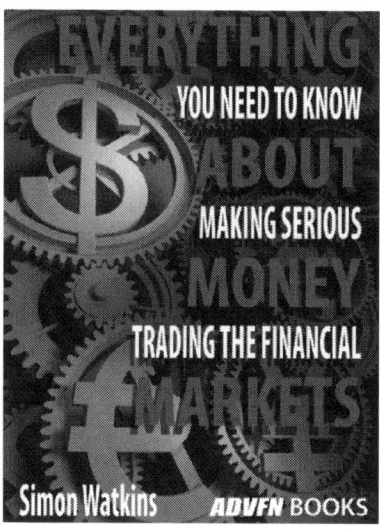

All over the world, people are trading on the financial markets. Some of them make a fortune – and many more lose their shirts. This book tells you how to be one of the winners.

It's a stark and sobering fact that around 90% of retail traders lose all of their trading money within about 90 days. That's because they have little grasp of the realities, technicalities, psychology and nature of the financial markets. In short, they don't know what they are doing.

*Everything You Need To Know About Making Serious Money Trading The Financial Markets* teaches you how to avoid being one of the 90%, and explains how to stack the odds firmly in your favour so you can become one of the 10% that make life-changing money trading. It's a trading bible that covers all aspects of the subject, from the psychology of trading and the mindset you need to succeed, through the fundamental principles that should guide your trades, to the trading methodologies that will help you succeed.

Fully illustrated with detailed charts, the book shows how you can use technical analysis to make your decisions, how to manage your risk and how to take out hedge positions to offset possible losses.

# MORE BOOKS FROM ADVFN

# 101 Charts for Trading Success

**by Zak Mir**

Using insider knowledge to reveal the tricks of the trade, Zak Mir's *101 Charts for Trading Success* explains the most complex set ups in the stock market.

Providing a clear way of predicting price action, charting is a way of making money by delivering high probability percentage trades, whilst removing the need to trawl through company accounts and financial ratios.

Illustrated with easy to understand charts this is the accessible, essential guide on how to read, understand and use charts, to buy and sell stocks. *101 Charts* is a must for all future investment millionaires.

# The Game in
# Wall Street

## by Hoyle and Clem Chambers

As the new century dawned, Wall Street was a game and the stock market was fixed. Ordinary investors were fleeced by big institutions that manipulated the markets to their own advantage and they had no comeback.

*The Game in Wall Street* shows the ways that the titans of rampant capitalism operated to make money from any source they could control. Their accumulated funds gave the titans enormous power over the market and allowed them to ensure they won the game.

Traders joining the game without knowing the rules are on a road to ruin. It's like gambling without knowing the rules and with no idea of the odds.

*The Game in Wall Street* sets out in detail exactly how this market manipulation works and shows how to ride the price movements and make a profit.

And guess what? The rules of the game haven't changed since the book was first published in 1898. You can apply the same strategies in your own investing and avoid losing your shirt by gambling against the professionals.

Illustrated with the very first stock charts ever published, the book contains a new preface and a conclusion by stock market guru Clem Chambers which put the text in the context of how Wall Street operates today.

# The Death of Wealth

### by Clem Chambers

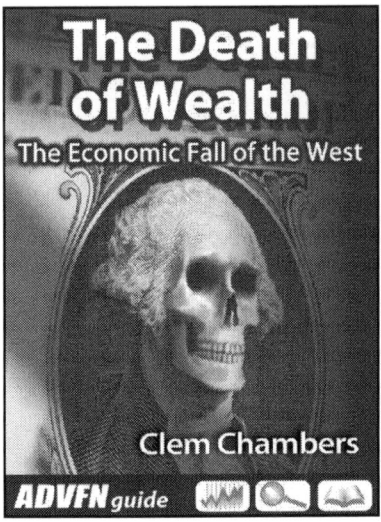

Question: what is the next economic game changer?
Answer: The Death of Wealth.

Market guru Clem Chambers dissects the global economy and the state of the financial markets and lays out the evidence for the death of wealth.

*The Death of Wealth* flags up the milestones on the route towards impending financial disaster. From the first tentative signs of recovery in the UK and US stock markets at the start of 2012, to the temporary drawing back from the edge of the Fiscal Cliff at the end, the book chronicles the trials and tribulations of the markets throughout the year.

Collecting together articles and essays throughout the last twelve months along with extensive new analysis for 2013, *The Death of Wealth* allows us to look at these tumultuous events collectively and draw a strong conclusion about what the future holds.

2012 started with the US economy showing signs of recovery, and European financial markets recovering some of the ground lost during the euro crisis. It ended with Obama's re-election and the deal that delayed the plunge off the fiscal cliff by a few months.

In between, the eurozone crisis continued, but none of the affected countries actually left the eurozone; quantitative easing tried to turn things around with the consequences of these "unorthodox" actions yet unknown; and the equity markets after the mid-year correction became strongly bullish.

*The Death of Wealth* takes you through the events of 2012 month by month, with charts showing the movements of the FTSE 100, the NASDAQ COMPX and the SSE COMPX throughout the year.

With an introduction by renowned market commentator and stock tipster Tom Winnifrith and a summary by trading technical analyst Zak Mir, this collection chronicles the rocky road trip the financial systems of the world have been on and predicts the ultimate destination: the death of wealth as we know it.

For more information go to the ADVFN Books website at www.advfnbooks.com.

**ADVFN BOOKS**

Printed in Great Britain
by Amazon